# ASPECTS OF LANGUAGE AND
# LANGUAGE TEACHING

# ASPECTS
# OF LANGUAGE AND
# LANGUAGE TEACHING

*by* W. A. BENNETT

CAMBRIDGE
AT THE UNIVERSITY PRESS
1969

Published by the Syndics of the Cambridge University Press
Bentley House, 200 Euston Road, London, N.W.1
American Branch: 32 East 57th Street, New York, N.Y. 10022

© Cambridge University Press 1968

Library of Congress Catalogue Card Number: 68–11280

Standard Book Number: 521 04164 3

First published 1968
Reprinted 1969

Printed in Great Britain
at the University Printing House, Cambridge
(Brooke Crutchley, University Printer)

# CONTENTS

# ILLUSTRATIONS

# ACKNOWLEDGEMENTS

A book of this kind brings its author into many fields of interest. I am grateful for the ready advice I have had from colleagues within these specialisations. Nevertheless, of course, I have sole responsibility for the result.

To my wife my thanks for her patient work in seeing the manuscript into typescript and for her tactful remonstrations when the complexities of my expression plunged the ideas into obscurity. Finally, to Joanne and Geoffrey, unceasing and largely uncontrolled generators.

# SIGNS USED IN THIS BOOK

⊖   is the sign for zero.

/ /   Phonetic symbols shown between pairs of oblique lines are being used phonemically (as described in chapter 2).

*   is used to indicate a malformation of language which is being used in illustration.

# INTRODUCTION

In the past few years there have been many books which have reflected in some way the new approach to language teaching. The most practical of them have viewed the language laboratory and its implications for all language teaching or have considered a number of scattered points in the language teaching situation, but with no attempt to gather the new teachings of linguistic and psychological theory into a unity governed by the practical day-to-day needs of the teacher.

I am attempting in this book to fill in the linguistic and psychological background. I should also like to suggest its relevance to the teaching situation and its usefulness to the teacher and administrator in further investigation or discussion. To the complete outsider the situation in descriptive linguistics and learning psychology must appear very confusing indeed, since it includes much of the marginal and eccentric work which is always part of total human endeavour and which the historical view will eventually allow us to ignore.

It is already possible to discern the important trends in both linguistics and psychology. One can also add a further selectivity by starting from the viewpoint of the language teacher. Feelings run high among the advocates of various linguistic and psychological theories, and the alarms and excursions deep inside the respective territories are many and fierce. Nevertheless, it is clear that what the language teacher can usefully learn from each of these two disciplines coincides with what will be the dominating lines of thought for a long time to come.

This book attempts to present a unified picture of the directions taken by contemporary language teaching and the attendant disciplines. Persuasion forms no part of its purpose, although the strength of my beliefs and prejudices no doubt occasionally shows through on some topics. Nevertheless, the selection of these topics, their arrangement and illustration, have been subject to as much objectivity as I can muster. I have been helped considerably in this by the problems and worries which have been put to me in recent years by teachers and those concerned with their training.

One great advantage of the new theories and methods is that they bring a great deal of objectivity into many parts of the language teaching process. I hope that this book may strengthen some teachers' understanding and support of the new techniques. It may even start some teachers on the road to conversion. Conversions in the other direction will be scarcely less welcome, but people holding contending views will find the discussion in language teacher organisations much more valuable and far less irritating if they know the framework of their discussion and can take the short cuts offered by a shared terminology.

A large part of discussion and argument amongst language teachers at the moment is vitiated by the absence of such common ground and by the need to define terms. Moreover, much time is wasted in talk amongst teachers by the tacit assumption that 'cultural' aspects of their job have an overriding importance. This book will be raising a functionalist banner. Perhaps this banner will eventually be shot down and language teaching return refreshed to the provision of tours of the great minds of other lands. The air will be that much clearer when the teacher is sure where his first responsibilities lie, and when he knows that his colleagues accept or reject this *explicitly*, and in what terms they do so.

Many new factors are bound to have a considerable effect on the work of language teachers. The teacher is used to having his textbook chosen for him, but the provision of ambitious equipment and taped or filmed material is going to place much heavier demands on him. Many teachers already know the feeling of being endowed with a language laboratory as though it were the equivalent of new blackboards throughout the school or college. No consultation, no thoroughgoing instruction, no explanation, just a huge piece of equipment with a capital and recurrent expenditure which *demands* some results. In the same way audio-visual and audio-lingual course material will become available, and no doubt further complex equipment will be added. The language teacher will be consulted on the design and adoption of material and equipment only if he has a clear professional doctrine on these matters, and such a creed can only come through efficient discussion with colleagues in language teacher associations.

The language teacher is likely to find the psychologist and the general linguist actively concerned in the construction and validation of teaching material. Too often the language teacher takes up, at the approach of experts, a defensive attitude which suggests uncertainty about his craft. The trained and moderately successful language teacher is a skilled craftsman and applies what the psychologist and descriptive linguist are concerned to describe in formal terms. These descriptions may offer important suggestions towards increased efficiency in his teaching but they deal merely with aspects of the teacher's activity. As such they are within the teacher's compass and fully within his understanding. Let the teacher remember that however esoteric they appear, linguistic descriptions are dealing with language as *he* knows it (although in a way which will include the less-familiar non-European languages in the theory), and the psychological theories of learning with the way *his* pupils learn and behave. Whether he adopts the descriptions and theories or not is for his professional conscience to judge. Understanding of the specialist pronouncements is essential to this judgment, but such understanding will depend on his willingness to suspend disbelief for a while.

There are no footnotes here, and references in the text to other works are very few. The book is intended to present the picture in its true simplicity, without the academic complexities of inbreeding. The bibliography contains the most pertinent books on the various topics dealt with in each chapter. It would be reasonable to treat the books listed as a basic reading list for all language teachers. Each book on the list, of course, has its own bibliography and in this way the reader can follow up his own particular interests in language and language teaching.

NOTE. The greatest difficulty that faces any attempt to describe a language is that it has to use for expression the very material that is being described. The weaknesses in such a situation are obvious and the modern descriptive linguist has for this reason taken procedures long known to logic and mathematics. However, unlike the logician and mathematician, the linguist is using these devices as an expedient and is constantly testing his statements by clothing them in words and trying them out on himself and other speakers of the language. Nevertheless, the reader who long ago turned his back on the mathematical may find some difficulty in following some of the descriptions of language structure. I hope he will persist, indeed part of my object has been to show that $A + B + C$ or $x \times y \times z$ is a reasonable way of showing what there is in common between sentences like 'he smiled quietly'; 'the doors opened wide'; 'happiness fades too soon' and avoids the prejudices and emotional charge of *words*. I have tried to make the introduction to the 'metalanguage' of descriptive linguistics a smooth and pleasant one. Any reader who experiences difficulty with the more complex symbol-systems will find it repays him to seek the guidance of a mathematician. He will be in that much better a position to judge the work of the linguistic sciences.

# 1. LANGUAGE

Language is the most distinctive of human activities. It is difficult
to disentangle the components because they spill over into human
personality itself. Many attempts have been made to define language,
and some definitions are highly complex. None but the simplest,
however, give a satisfactory definition since intuition must play a
large part in the recognition of language.

As a starting-point, language may be thought of in broad terms
as having many of the characteristics of a code. As such it depends
on the tacit agreement between speaker (or writer) and listener (or
reader) that a set of signs, more or less systematised, shall have
certain references. If I say or write 'kailorgo' it will mean nothing
to you unless you and I (or our parents—or their parents) have
agreed that this shall refer to my going out of the house, opening
the garage doors, getting into the car and moving it forward by use
of the engine and the controls. 'I'll get the car out' only refers to
a similar sequence of events because it has been agreed that such
is the happening to which this set of noises or scratches will refer.

The difficulty in stating these references is that many of them
have not been made explicit. The references or 'meaning' of the
noises or scratches are related to the accumulation of past events,
of past and present personal or communal experience. A dictionary
may make these references appear to be firm and definable, which
is misleading; a thesaurus will more honestly state them in their
relationships. No word is fully explicable, because its range of
reference is defined by an interplay of central or explicit meaning,
the recent and distant experience of the community, the experiences
of the individual, the personality of the speaker. It will also be defined by the identity of the person spoken or written to, by the
circumstances and social position of those in communication and
so on. This would all be very confusing and would defeat comprehension if each user of this 'code' were not just a little uncertain
about some of these attendant facts. Much of the time he will be
dealing with people he has not met before or meets only seldom.
He will therefore rely on the agreed part of the reference system,
roughly what would be stated by a dictionary for a given word.
Simply because of this, it is possible to learn one's native language
or a foreign language rather than having to demand for each
occasion the establishment of a fresh *ad hoc* code. But the dictionary
will help me little in understanding and using appropriately

'walk' in such ways as 'I've just come back from a five mile walk' or 'He comes from a different walk of life' or 'He had a curious walk' or 'That postman's walk has too many tall houses on it'. Such examples make it clear, of course, that the word is not really fundamental in language but I shall want to return to this in a later chapter.

A language in the full speech-community will be used in such a way that the references may be assumed to be known to the listener or correspondent (or explanatory remarks will be included). A speaker may say 'She's got a wonderful bust' and add hurriedly 'the one of Socrates, in her dining room' but of course the context, the previous conversation, the speaker's knowledge of the person to whom he is talking would make the references of what is said perfectly clear in the first place. In a closed speech-community, such as a gang, a school, a club, a regiment or a profession, language can be less explicit still. The very fact that communication is between the members of a close community means that certain things can be taken for granted about experience and attitudes. In the same way, dialect words or technical words can have a more closely delimited reference than they would have in the larger community simply because they are used in a particular kind of context. Everyone will have experienced the irritation caused when it is wrongly assumed that the listener or reader is a member of a particular speech-group or when a teenager makes no effort to clarify items in his code.

Language is clearly a kind of code, but, just as clearly, there are other codes that no-one would consider as language. Most of these, such as the morse code, semaphore or military codes have a consistent reference to a particular language. The items in one of these codes are merely different expressions or *exponents* of an existing language and only have 'meaning' as they represent that language. No questions of style could ever arise, and there can be little expression of personality and no representation of new objects or ideas *within* the code. Firm conclusions as to style, personality or neologism would be possible only when the direct referents in the base language were known. The secondary system (the code) would merely require to be transliterated—'knee' would be represented by four symbols regardless of the uselessness of any of them and no suggestion of 'meaning' could exist without the possibility of transliteration. Military and business codes require a somewhat more complex replacement. Terseness is usually important, so the relation is likely to be that of one code word representing a complete language phrase or an even larger unit.

Such codes, coming nearer to a relationship of symbol to idea ('triumph' in a code might mean 'the deal has been successfully concluded', 'we've sold the generator', 'I've signed the contract'), may come to play a direct part in communication, with direct reference to an idea. This is the way that technical expressions, which may originally have been part of a code, come into the language—'a bear market', 'zero hour'. Codes of this kind are designed to refer to a specific field of activity and are usually intended to maintain secrecy. They are doubly vulnerable since the items must change as circumstances change, for they lack the considerable flexibility of real language items, and they must be entirely replaced when security is in doubt. Both of these considerations will usually militate against complexity of coding, as will considerations of the speed of encoding and decoding.

Language is a code to the extent that it is a symbolisation of the phenomena of existence and imagination. It is more than a code because it is capable of change to meet new circumstances and to express variations of individual personality. How far these variations can go will depend on the nature of the 'norm' language and a number of other factors.

We each have access to more than one version of our own native language. There is the standard language of the community, which is enshrined in dictionary, grammar, thesaurus, the distillation of the best writers. It may be my teachers' precepts and my elders' example. The standard language may be a medley of items used by one (dominant) social class or a dialect which has reached a position of dominance for various social or cultural reasons. There may indeed be no one variety felt to be standard, and communication within the community will depend on a considerable degree of tolerance of variant forms and meanings. In these circumstances it is likely that feelings of national unity will often be at a low ebb, unless there are other, strong factors supporting feelings of nationalism. Indeed, where such feelings exist the tendency will be strongly in favour of the development of a standard language.

The community's language will act as a point of reference for all the members of the community who accept such membership. I, as a speaker of English, am concerned to identify myself as a member of that community. I am also determined to communicate with other members of the community. It is, therefore, essential that I remain sufficiently close to what I *feel* to be the standard norm of English to ensure that I am accepted and understood by these fellow-members of the community. As a Briton, I am helped in this by hearing my contemporaries and by such voices of authority as the B.B.C.

Nevertheless I am also concerned to express my personality and to communicate ideas and needs which I am sure must be different from others' needs and concepts. And so there must be this continual compromise between the language which supplies my need to communicate, on condition that I more or less conform, and the language which will express my uniqueness and the uniqueness of my situation.

My personal language is free to vary within the limits of acceptability and reference to the communal norm-language. All the members of a community must engage in this compromise or resign from the community in some respect. Basically, it is a simple two-pole choice. Too great a departure from the neighbourhood of the norm-language leads to unintelligibility and that is permitted only to the insane or to the poet. It is customary for society to make an effort to understand certain poets, and psychiatrists are leading the interest in the language of insanity.

Intelligibility normally presents few difficulties in our native language. Training, education, reading, listening, have all contributed to train us in making ourselves understood. Moreover, when we speak we usually have a quick reaction from another human being which tells us whether we have been understood or not. The absence of such an immediate feedback is what makes lecturing, broadcasting and writing particularly difficult.

Acceptability of variations in the language of an individual or of a group within a community is subject to pressures and attitudes which are less than rational. There may be aesthetic criteria, or prestige may attach to one kind of language-variety because of an individual or event associated with it. One variety may be associated with a good education, another with a lack of education simply because tradition has led society to think that way. There are no *linguistic* reasons for the social prestige or disrepute in which varieties are held, provided that full communication is assured. There is no *linguistic* justification for preferring ' I like unsalted butter' to ' I likes unsal'ed bu''er'. Nor is there any linguistic reason for preferring 'It was utterly splendid' pronounced with an Oxford accent to 'Was smashin'' with an East London accent. Any preferences of this kind will be entirely subjective, based on one's musical sense, one's respect for the subjective dogmatic statements of grammarians, one's liking or detestation of associations with the particular variety. A Devonian or a Texan may be almost incomprehensible and may come near to breaking the first rule for membership of a speech-community, by making communication almost impossible outside a region. Even so, the listener's liking for cream teas or for the Texan grandeur may well be sufficient to make the particular variety not only acceptable but even preferable to a more easily understood variety. Such individual or group varieties of language may acquire and lose prestige for a number of reasons which have nothing what-soever to do with language itself.

If a community is sufficiently conscious of its identity and of the norm-language which accompanies it, it may react quite violently to any variation. Individual variation may be tolerated, group varia-tion will scarcely ever be. Acceptability in this case will depend on the feelings of members of the community on finding an individual or group living amongst them and choosing not to conform. This is the obverse of the group's use of a language to identify itself and to act as a factor of unity between its members. The operation of these factors may be conscious or not, but they are likely to play a very important part in the linguistic life of a community. I will find acceptable the language of a member of my central group within the community, I will also find acceptable a large number of varia-tions from other parts of the community; I may not find so accept-able the language of the beatnik or the language of the docks, or the language of the racecourse—although I will tolerate them. It is certain that language will play a major part in the conformism to which each nation is moving.

There is, then, for each community one or more languages, each of which generates vocabulary and grammar. Each is a notional thing which exists only in so far as it permits each native of that speech-community to know intuitively if an item of vocabulary belongs to the possible inventory of the language. It will also enable the native to decide whether utterances, spoken or written, in the language are grammatical or not, or only partially so. This notional language may become partly explicit in the writings of prescriptive gram-marians, based on intuition and also on consciously applied prin-ciples drawn from the history or literature of the language or of other languages. In giving conscious expression to his intuitions the grammarian may often be led astray by logical or historical con-siderations which are no part of the language. Indeed he may well end up by pronouncing the 'It's me' as wrong because 'the verb "to be" governs a complement; a complement cannot be in an oblique case; "me" is the oblique form ("accusative" or "preposi-tional") and should therefore be replaced by "I"'. On historical grounds he might say that the first persons singular and plural of any verb are 'I should...', 'we should...' and that 'I would'/'we would' are wrong. He would be making these statements on grounds which are completely outside contemporary language; imposing an analysis drawn in the one case from other languages, in the other case from older texts. If he were to ask a native speaker of English to pronounce on which was 'English', one who had not been taught to think like the particular grammarian, he would undoubtedly be told that 'It's me' and 'I would think so' are preferable to 'It's I' and 'I should think so', although he would probably be told that the latter was also acceptable.

The nature of the speaker's intuition (his *competence*) is certainly not really understood, yet it is clearly in action whenever a native of the speech-community rejects an utterance as 'not English', 'a bit strange', 'foreign, somehow', 'not good grammar', although the last remark probably comes from someone who is conscious of a grammarian's or a schoolmaster's statements. This person will often be one who can be heard to say 'It's him' and yet to reject it in favour of 'It's he' when others use it.

The expression of the notional language takes place, as the result of intuition, whenever an utterance occurs. The utterance is the individual use of language by the members of a community. The notional language presents limits within which grammatical or vocabulary items are felt to be acceptable. These limits are sufficiently vague to allow the poet and the orator to overstep them occasionally without being accused of being 'foreign'. There are occasions, too, when these limits are so vague that uncertainty sets in and the answer supplied by the grammarian is felt to be as good as any.

Well within these limits, however, the individual is theoretically free to construct his utterances and to select vocabulary as he chooses. But language does more than encode communication. There is also the identifying function of language in operation to which I have already referred. Language offers a signalling system which can be put to many uses over and above the encoded information content.

I may identify myself as belonging to a particular speech-community or to a group within that community. The group may be inclusive or exclusive, open or closed. If I am British I may, for prestige purposes, choose to suggest an American origin, and vice versa, or I may compromise by adopting a 'midatlantic' pronunciation, a blend suggesting that I originate from both England and the United States, travelling regularly from one to the other, and having my home just off the west coast of Ireland. On the other hand, I may wish to have entry to a restricted group and I shall prepare myself by using the right vocabulary and using certain grammatical constructions favoured by the fortunate members of the group to which I aspire. In England the group is well prepared for a change of social class by an individual when he adopts a new 'language'—a new 'accent'—the right vocabulary, the most frequent grammatical features. Of course there is more to it than just language, which is only part of the total behaviour. Yet language is usually the most identifiable feature of a co-religionist, a political sympathiser, an advertising man. It has been said that half the qualification of a sociologist is to know the right terms, and recognition as a linguist may well depend on a correct use of the attendant language!

Groups may be social or professional, religious or political. The total of these groups and of the few determined individualists is the total activity of the community, and the distillation of this activity will be added to the community's cultural heritage. Language and culture are interrelated in such a highly complex manner that they are easily taken as identical. Culture is, however, a reflexion of the total behaviour of a society, or of that section which has dominance or which is admired by the others; as such it is not identical with language. This statement, of course, immediately puts in question the position and aims of language teaching, a subject which will be the concern of a later chapter. The handling of cultural tradition has been one of the most important rôles of language, and notably written language. There is now a greater variety of methods for recording and handing on our own and future cultures. Film and video-tape recording will complement language in this task of handing on cultural consciousness.

The nature of 'culture' and its form in the future is beyond the scope of this book. The diminished importance of the prescriptive approach to language, and the recognition of social class or caste language as simply a variety alongside professional or sectionalist varieties, are factors which will undoubtedly support a broadening of the cultural tradition to reflect the activity of the whole community.

The activity of a community, and even the community itself, is shaped by politics and religion. Language is closely interrelated with these two facets of communal life. The practitioners of both are often outstanding manipulators of language, and a decline of public interest in both can be explained partly by the scarcity of great exponents of language within these fields.

Historically, religion has been the source of much of the total of cultural items which have come to us. In the religious use of language there has been an association of mystic significance with language in which its communicating function has often come to be replaced by a system of symbols with magical properties. In time the same language has been used as support of the exclusiveness of a social/professional group, the priesthood. A language has often been conserved in this function until the gap between it and the vulgar language, the sum of the individual languages of the excluded, has grown wide enough to separate two distinct languages. Indeed a foreign language has often been introduced to a community in association with a new faith or creed. The influence exerted by the foreign language because of its association with mystic activities has been less strong than in societies where the two have been closely related. Thus the significance of the Latin of Roman Catholicism will have been quite different, and linguistically more important, in Italy or France than in the Roman Catholic parts of Germany or Holland. Where the language of religion is indigenous enough to be more or less understood by the people and yet old enough to maintain its distance by its strangeness of forms, the religion may be sure of a place in the mystic consciousness of the community; the language will make it something related but different. Where, as in England, the language of Catholicism and the established church faces a vulgar tongue completely different from the language of its religious origins there is a choice between communication and the loss of the strangeness which can give a poetic edge to belief. This compromise between communication and an avoidance of the workaday associations of the community's language is seen most clearly where, as in England, the forms of language adopted two or three centuries ago, as a defiant gesture in support of clarity and honesty of belief, are retained in parts of the service in spite of the development of modern English, because they lend a patina to belief and worship. The excluding rôle of language is nowhere stronger than in a society's search for a declaration of its identity. The stresses and strains of nationality are sharpened by the nature of the codes used within its geographical limits. The variation which is bound to exist between the varieties of language used by groups making up the larger community does much to blur the situation and to encourage a degree of tolerance of divergences from what may be regarded by any one group as the norm. Such tolerance may extend to one or two groups using languages fairly closely related to the norm or, for historical and other reasons, to a comparatively small group speaking a very different language. The larger community is hardly likely to tolerate any growth in the use of these different codes or the introduction of any further large variations unless the other conditions are unusually favourable. The problem is likely to be most acute at or near frontiers, where the community's identity is likely to be less certain.

It may well be that tolerance of sub-communities using a different language may increase as a result of increased travel and greater familiarity with other language-communities. Nevertheless, there are frequently dramatic reminders of the importance attached to a national language in the context of other dangers felt by substantial groups within the community.

Conflict is likely where language differences and differences of belief run parallel. In Belgium there is the added provocation of a parallelism between political and religious beliefs, but even there the clearest marker of all these differences is the differences in language, and it easily becomes the very symbol of dissension. A similar situation exists in India but with the added complication that a multiplicity of unrelated languages has made of English, a foreign language with imperialist associations, the only readymade *lingua franca*.

The needs both of communication and of identification favour the adoption or imposition of a national language where large groups within a nation use widely disparate languages and where none is dominant. Of course, it may not be possible to decide on one language as a dominant one; and, as in the case of Switzerland, the existence of a number of languages side by side may be part of a community's very nationhood. The maintenance of a number of languages in a state of equality of regard is an expensive decision for a community, for it increases administrative and educational costs and places an extra linguistic burden on its members, particularly those striving to achieve prominence at a national level.

Normally, however, the languages and varieties of languages within a community do not exist in a state of equilibrium. The dynamic nature of language will ensure the dominance of one language, and of one variety of it over all the others. Such dominance may be the result of the importance of industry or literary production in one region, of the influence of institutions or individuals in some sphere of national life. It may be the result of linguistic considerations: one writing system may be easier to convert to print or may be shared with other important trading or otherwise influential nations; one spoken language may likewise be related to the languages of certain important nations.

External forces may well lead to the dominance of one of the native languages; it is more likely to be internal conditions which favour the adoption of one dialect of the particular native language. Trade, the handing on of legends, political movements, the development of the educational system, these and other down-to-earth factors will lead to the dominance of one regional language. At the same time a group within the community will be associated with success and will exercise both attraction and exclusiveness. This group's language may well come to be dominant or play a large part in the amalgam eventually adopted by the nation.

Political control and language are often closely related. A language can play a central part in the establishment of a national consciousness and its use may well be fostered by the proponents of a nationhood. The Welsh and Irish languages are closely associated with the fostering of a national consciousness, and this is true of languages in many other communities.

The development of a national language may be encouraged where the resultant proto-nation is an administratively viable unit. On the other hand, the strengthening of regional and local languages may be undertaken to the detriment of any one national language when the larger community might be politically unstable. This has been a deliberate policy in the Soviet Union, and is clearly a part of other large communities where the facts of the society run counter to the development of a stable nation. The facts here are interestingly reversed when the written language is utterly separate from the spoken, as in the case of Chinese. The so-called 'dialects' of spoken Chinese are by any linguistic definition separate languages, being mutually unintelligible. The written language is unaffected by these differences and serves as a unifying factor. Moreover, whereas most important writing systems are related to spoken language, Chinese retains an ideographic system in which many symbols have a conceptual significance rather than a linguistic one. The unifying factor, therefore, offers a conceptual patterning at the same time that it performs a linguistic function.

We have been considering language principally at the level of the total society rather than its use at the level of the individual. In this way we have been dealing with an idea rather than a reality. A language is, in reality, the sum total of all the individual codes which are recognised as being within the confines of acceptability. This is vague, but it is less misleading than to refer to language as though it were a clearly-defined and integrated phenomenon. 'Language' is certainly as 'real' as 'chair leg', and, as such, may be described as though it really exists as a static whole. It may have qualities ascribed to it which are relevant at a certain abstract level but are meaningless at the molecular level. The difference between 'language' and 'chair leg' is that 'a chair leg' may be used and known 'in toto', whereas one (individual's) English from the class 'English' can never be known except by guesswork extension from what we hear or read of the individual's English to a whole system which we could then describe as his (imagined) 'English'. In the world of the chair leg it would be like sitting on a chair supported by parts of chair legs but successfully supported because we have faith in the existence of the rest of the chair leg.

We may for most practical purposes leave the most individual use of language (*idiolect*) to the psychologist and the poet. The language specialist is primarily concerned with language as a communicating mechanism and is, therefore, interested in its group use. Whether the group is large or small, socially important or not, will affect not the linguistic but the sociological analysis and will be an important concern in language teaching. Linguistic investigation will normally concern itself at the level of the group, defined traditionally in terms of geography (*dialect*). There is growing tendency for linguistic investigation to concern itself with the operational use of language in performing certain social functions or maintaining social rather than geographical groupings (*register*).

The difference between a dialect and a language can usually only be defined, if at all, in terms of geography; a dialect being restricted by geographical limitations, a language being accepted by a number of dialect groups and being used throughout a (political) region or nation. It is clearly easier to recognise a language or a dialect as such than to offer a definition or even to state the reasons for the difference. It seems as though it will be easier and more useful to set up definitions of language varieties in terms of function. Not only are geographical differences bound to decrease in importance, but a functional definition of register will offer both a definition of a code in social terms and will, at the same time, offer a current rather than historical statement of the reasons for the difference.

Whilst the mapping out of *isoglosses*, lines marking places where the same linguistic forms are to be found, and the establishment of dialect geographies is comparatively well-developed, work on the description of language functions at a fairly delicate, group-level is quite recent. It is unlikely, of course, that the two will be mutually exclusive. At an agricultural market the functional language is likely to coincide with the local dialect and the same is true of the registers used by industrial workers. Entertainers, too, may work with a particular dialect, singers using a different one from comedians; music-hall comedians using yet a different one from radio and television comedians. The same influences as are at work in establishing the dominant rôle played by a language or a dialect may well be in action in fostering the use of one dialect or of a consciously or unconsciously created variant as the vehicle for a particular group in a particular function.

A large part of the differences displayed by differences of register will be a result of differences in the use of words in the language, or *lexical* use, lexical items to express needs and experiences unique to the activity or range of activities in question. The part played by grammar and pronunciation has yet to be fully described but it is certain that, for instance, scientists prefer passive forms and impersonal structures: 'it has been ascertained that...' rather than 'I (or he or you) have found that...'. Moreover, most people can identify a 'way of saying things' or 'a kind of voice' typical of the priest or the schoolmaster, the cricket commentator or the policeman. This identification, too, is still possible even when the content is not clear, suggesting that identity of *function* is signalled at least partly by features of pronunciation alone.

Language is a kind of code and so rests on an essentially arbitrary relationship of symbol and concept. For centuries this relationship was regarded as being far closer and, often, as having mystic significance. The relationship is now recognised as a compound of tradition and situation. The term 'context of situation' was first used by Malinowski in an essay appended to *The Meaning of Meaning*. The relative importance of language and situation varies. In formal written language the situation will have no importance and the language as scratched out in marks on paper will have to carry all the meaning. At the other extreme two friends may have no need of language but may rely on their knowledge of each other and the import of the situation to communicate by a facial expression, by a gesture or by silence alone. In this last example, of course, language is inoperative. However, a grunt or a sigh would fulfil the conditions for language to be held as operating: there would be noise which was part of a system (deep grunts; nasal grunts; long sighs; short sighs) and the kind of noise made would contrast the situation with a similar but completely silent situation.

In this example the unit of 'language', here a noise made as alternative to all other possible noises within the same system, provided the minimum change of meaning, given that there was a change, however small, in the significance of the situation. One operational way of defining language is, then, to regard it as part of a situational whole. In our example the introduced grunt or sigh (language) acted as the only variable since the rest of the situation remained unchanged. It would be possible, on the other hand, to introduce one utterance in the language consistently into a variety of situations and to ask a group of native speakers of the language to judge whether the utterance would be acceptable in each of the situations. In this way it would be possible to suggest the range of availability of the utterance, thus providing a more accurate assessment of meaning than is available from any other source. The dictionary, after all, merely states possible replacement utterances (= 'equivalents' or 'definitions') available for certain situations. The dictionary is always unreliable to the extent that it fails to indicate the range of use of the words and phrases and, therefore, implies that the utterance and its substitute are coextensive.

The trouble is that language is far more complex than any example can suggest, and the whole of communication is of a far greater complexity still. The last section might have implied that language is in simple opposition to silence. Communication, of course, is made up of utterances of all kinds, and of silences too. The pause is linguistic and is a unit of pronunciation. 'And then he spoke...!' is clearly different in meaning from 'And then he spoke!'. The spoken language has a far greater range of pregnant silences available than the sequence of dots or the dash which may be the mark of reference to a situation—the pause.

Any analysis of situations would present us with a continuous line stretching from background to noise or gestures, with language and context merging almost indissolubly in the areas of intonation, stress, pauses and those splutters and coughs which are generally classed as paralinguistic features.

For the sake of simplicity I have largely ignored the written language. Any book written about language fifty years ago, or even more recently, would certainly have dealt in terms of the written language and have made scant reference to the spoken language. It is significant of the new approach that I should have given most attention to the rôle of spoken language and have referred only fleetingly to the written forms.

The written language has usually the prestige associated with history and tradition. Mystic significance was usually attached to the scratches of language, not to the phonic substance. Writing, being a skill acquired later than speech, came to be associated with educational achievement, and the comparative permanence of written as against oral literature led to a greater value being attached to the graphic substance of language. All these factors have obscured the greater variety and expressiveness of the spoken language. It is far more vital than its equivalent written form, but was far more ephemeral until the arrival of sound recording.

Modern linguistics, as we shall see, works first with the range of spoken language and treats the written language as one variety, perhaps the most prestigious, yet only one variety of the language. Graphic substance, writing, is the parallel of phonic substance, speech, but can move only, as it were, horizontally. Poets have occasionally tried to vary the plane in which it moves by introducing symbols, different typefaces, symbolic shaping of lines of verse. Essentially pictographic scripts like Chinese have an added dimension. That the spoken language always exists at more complex levels we shall see in chapter 2.

## 2. LINGUISTICS

In the first chapter we considered the function of language, in this chapter we shall be concerned with its nature. In the first chapter, too, we considered language principally as an idea rather than through its actual exponents.

We have, nevertheless, seen that language exists at three levels. There is first of all the ideal; what we mean, for instance, when we talk about the 'German language' or the 'Russian language', with no thought for the diverse dialect and idiolect forms which go to make up this amalgam, one which is never to be found in any part of Germany or the Soviet Union. Even if, as sometimes happens, 'German' or 'Russian' is equated with the language as used in one specific region, this is still an idealisation, for nowhere will there be a consistent exposition of the ideal by native users from that region.

Language in use tolerates considerable divergence among speakers. The sum of the divergences in use by those accepted as native speakers constitutes a second level. Whatever these divergences, shared features operate at a degree of efficiency sufficient for other members of the speech-community. Communication is not by any means the sole criterion and indeed may be only a minor fact in the native speaker's judgment of another's performance. Communication between the Londoner and the Cornishman may be difficult, but geographical and political considerations will offset these difficulties sufficiently for each to consider the other as performing within the outline of possibilities constituting 'English'. On the other hand, some speakers on one side of the Austro-German frontier or of the Atlantic might consider speakers on the other side to be unacceptably divergent in their performance, although few differences of any importance might exist in their use of language.

Within this second level of language an individual speaker's performance will depend on many factors: the linguistic influences on him as a result of (*a*) the social groups, and (*b*) the geographical areas to which he has belonged at various times in his life; conscious or unconscious acceptance or rejection of tendencies or fashions in the language he feels to be his own; physical limitations resulting in the inability to discriminate certain sounds or certain signs, or the inability to articulate certain sounds or to compose certain signs (these limitations exist within the bounds of 'normality'); his conscious or unconscious rôle-playing. The individual's language may vary from day to day depending on all these factors and their interrelationship. Whatever the linguistic performance, it must remain within the limits accepted by the other members of the immediate speech-community (who in turn must perform within these limits) if the speaker is not to court the consequences of exclusion, good or bad, which were considered in chapter 1.

Because the French linguist, Fernand de Saussure, was the first to specify these three states of language, it is customary to use, respectively, the French words *langue* (the imaginary ideal), *langage* (actual variations within the confines of the ideal), and *parole* (idiolect). For practical reasons descriptive linguists normally concern themselves with *langage* alone. Individual use of language (parole), the speech act, is affected by many non-linguistic features. As de Saussure wrote: 'L'activité du sujet parlant doit être étudiée dans un ensemble de disciplines qui n'ont de place dans la linguistique que par leurs relations avec la langue.' Many of the features are so personal that they are beyond measurement or description, or more likely to be the concern of the speech therapist, the sociologist and psychologist than of the linguistic scientist. And yet, of course, that language which is the concern of the linguist exists in the total of these individual speech acts. The linguist beginning work on the description of a language indeed works with *informants*, i.e. individual speakers of the language, though of course he works towards what are essentially abstractions from a number of these individual performances. Some of the latest descriptive investigations of language use are working on the basis of individual use within well-defined social groups. The descriptive linguist working with material provided by individual informants is dealing with *parole*. He can only hope that the range of his informants will have some statistical validity. To complete the description he will need to test it on the speech acts of a further range of native speakers.

The *langue*, then, is expounded as *langage* which is the sum of the individual acts of language (*parole*). Its exposition will certainly be in organised sound ('phonic substance') and probably in systematised marks on paper or other material ('graphic substance'). Whereas every language in the world uses sound produced by the individual with his body, many languages have no written form.

The range of phonic substance which the human being can produce by blocking or modifying in other ways the waste air as it is expelled from the body is enormous. Only a very small part of this potential range is ever used by any one language.

On the other hand, the range of graphic substance the normal individual is able to produce is bound to be very limited by comparison. Moreover, it lacks the freedom of the ephemeral speech act. Graphic substance is there for others to see and to judge. Its variation from the 'educated' or otherwise acceptable norm can be measured. The tendency for the written substance to conform will be very strong indeed. Divergence in one direction may be characterised as uneducated or subnormal, in another as artistic or abnormal.

Because of this permanence, the written language, where it exists, has tended to be taken as the norm, with the spoken language as a debased relative. There have been exceptions, when great actors and great orators were recognised, but great writers come more easily to mind.

It was clearly difficult to work with the spoken language before recording equipment became available, and even then the trained human ear was probably a better receiver than the earliest equipment. While the spoken word and the spoken sentence could be dealt with, no account could be taken of larger units of spoken sound, and little of fluent speech anyway. The effect of this on linguistic analysis can still be seen today. Most linguistic work is concerned with the 'sentence', very little with the 'paragraph'.

The greatest need was to establish a system of notation which could be used to record the sounds of speech. The International Phonetic Association was inaugurated in 1886 and its system of transcription, constantly improved, is recognised almost everywhere for the notation of spoken language. It will be used throughout this book whenever it becomes necessary to move away from the limitations of the conventional orthography. The pronunciation referred to in this book as English is that found amongst speakers in Southern England. In general terms it is similar to RP ('received pronuncia-

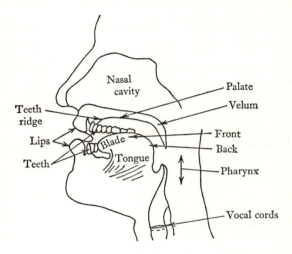

Fig. 1. Oral cavity showing relevant features.

tion') as described by Professor Daniel Jones in his *Outline of English Phonetics.*

The reader unfamiliar with phonetic transcription will need to refer to the listings of vowel and consonant values given on page 24. It should not prove difficult for the language specialist to learn their values sufficiently to recognise the significance of transcriptions used in this book. Moreover, the language teacher is strongly advised to follow up this aspect of language, for many topics in applied linguistics will, of necessity, be expressed in terms of phonetic notation when normal orthography will not serve. He would do well to invest the very small sum necessary to buy *The Principles of the International Phonetic Association* published in Great Britain by the Association at the Department of Phonetics, University College, London, w.c. 1.

This present book is *not* a reader in phonetics, but some acquaintance with the subject is essential in its bearing on the nature of language.

In very broad terms the air expelled by the body may be modified by the position of the tip, the blade or the body of the tongue in relation to the teeth, the alveolar ridges, the palate or the velum. It may be modified by the shape of the lips, the position of the velum, or by the degree of tension of the cheeks or of the vocal chords. If the vocal chords are brought loosely together, the air passing through the pharynx will bring them into vibration. The resulting sound may be said to have *voice*. If the air is not thus restricted the sound will be *voiceless*. Essentially this is the difference between English 'd' (voiced) and 't' (voiceless) as in o*dd*er/o*tt*er, b/p in ri*bb*ed/ri*pp*ed, g/k in sa*gg*ing/sa*ck*ing. Further modifications may take place in the mouth. If the velum is lowered and the mouth closed, the air is diverted through the nose and a *nasal* sound is produced as English 'n' in *n*ab. Contrast the pronunciation of the first sound in this word with the first sound in *d*ab. The major difference is the diversion of air from the mouth in *n*ab.

The tongue may act as the obstacle to the expended air. The tip or blade may touch the alveolar ridge to produce a dental sound as in English *d*on or may touch the teeth to produce French *d*onne. The front of the tongue may be raised towards the palate as in English *y*es, or the back may touch the velum as in English *c*art. It may be rolled as in the Scottish pronunciation of *r*um or it may be flapped as in Spanish pe*r*o. The tongue may obstruct the centre of the air passage so that air is forced out on either side of it (*lateral*) as in Welsh *ll*an (voiceless alveolar lateral fricative) or English *l*ate (voiced alveolar lateral non-fricative). The sound may be restricted by both lips (*bilabial*) as in English *p*in (voiceless), *b*in (voiced), *m*in (nasal). Where there is complete blockage of air as in *p*in, *b*in, *t*in, *d*in, *k*in, etc., there will be a mild expulsion of air upon release and such sounds are called *plosive*. The sounds in *p*in, *t*in, *k*ing can therefore be described, respectively, as bilabial, dental and velar voiceless plosives. A more delicate description is always possible. A textbook in phonetics would point out that English 'b', 'd' and 'g' are fully voiced only when they occur between vowels, and then not by all speakers!

When the sound is produced by air passing through a narrow gap between two organs of speech it is called a *fricative*. 'f' in English

| Consonants | Bilabial | Labio-dental | Dental and alveolar | Palato-alveolar | Palatal | Velar | Glottal |
|---|---|---|---|---|---|---|---|
| Plosive | p b | | t d | | | k g | ʔ |
| Nasal | m | | n | | | ŋ | |
| Lateral | | | l | | | | |
| Rolled, flapped or rolled fricative | | | r | | | | |
| Fricative | | f v | θ ð \| s z | ʃ ʒ | | | h |
| Frictionless continuants and semi-vowels | w \| y | | | | j | | |

| Vowels | | Front | Central | Back |
|---|---|---|---|---|
| Close | | i y | | u |
| Half-close | | e ø | | o |
| | | | ə | |
| Half-open | | ɛ œ | | ʌ ɔ |
| Open | | | a | |

Fig. 2. Classification of I.P.A. symbols by place and manner of the sounds to which they refer when used in this book.

*f*air (labiodental voiceless) and 'v' in *v*an (labiodental voiced) are examples of fricative sounds. So is 'th' in *th*in (dental voiceless fricative), 'th' in *th*en (dental voiced fricative), 's' in *s*oon, 'z' in *z*oom (respectively, alveolar voiceless and voiced fricatives), 'sh' in *sh*ore and the sound coinciding with 'si' in vi*si*on (Russian 'ж', French 'j' as in *j*ournal) respectively, palatoalveolar voiceless and voiced fricatives, 'h' (glottal fricative). There are many more combinations possible, but this description, like the table of symbols above and the list of symbols on page 24 is limited to sounds which will be used in this book.

Whereas consonants are produced by some degree of obstruction of the air passage, vowel sounds are produced by a much freer passage of voice. The various vowel sounds can be distinguished primarily by tongue positions within the mouth and secondarily by lip shape. The diagram on this page shows the symbols for what are known as the *cardinal vowels* set in positions corresponding to the approximate tongue position in a side view of the mouth. Also shown are the symbols for vowels produced with the same tongue positions but variations of lip position. These *secondary cardinal vowels* are limited to those which will be used in this book. The values of these vowel sounds are illustrated in the list on page 24. Vowel sounds may vary in length since the passage of air is not blocked. The sign ː is used to show length. The phonetic transcription of Southern English 'could' and 'cooed' is, respectively, /kud/ and /kuːd/, 'Sid' and 'seed' is respectively, /sid/ and /siːd/.

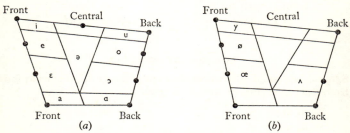

Fig. 3. Diagrams of tongue position. The sounds shown in *b* are produced with more lip-rounding.

As with consonants, the air may be diverted through the nose. This is marked by ˜ over a vowel. French 'gras' and 'grand' are transcribed respectively /gra/ and /grã/. Certain consonants may be formed with so much voice that they form a syllable by themselves. This is marked by ˌ under the symbol. Southern English pronunciation of 'garden' may be written as 'gaːdn̩/'.

It will be clear from what has been said about idiolect that a wide range of sounds will be produced in practice. For instance we may describe a sound as that produced by tongue in position *x*, lips forming shape *y*, and *z* quantity of voice being expelled. Each individual would vary each of these constituents to a certain extent. Acoustically the result would be measurably different, and yet the sound produced would be recognised as belonging to a certain sound 'class' in the language. The English or American pronunciation of

### VOWEL SYMBOLS

i   as in (Southern) English *bit*; also used for the sound in French *il*

| | |
|---|---|
| iː  as in *peak* | ɛ  as in *pen* |
| e  as in French *dé* | a  as in French *la* |
| aː  as in *park*; used also for French *gare* | |
| ɔ  as in *not* | œ  as in French *œuf* |
| ɔː  as in *nought* | ʌ  as in *cup* |
| o  as in French *peau* | ɷ  as in *book* |
| u  as in French *bout* | ə  as *a* in *attempt*; also |
| uː  as in *soon* |     used for the sound |
| y  as in French *rue* |     in French *le* |
| ø  as in French *peu* | əː  as in *girl* |

### CONSONANT SYMBOLS

Symbols are listed only where they are different in value or in form from the consonants of written English

| | |
|---|---|
| g  as in *get* | j  as *y* in *yet* |
| s  as in *see* | |
| ʔ  'glottal stop', as in German between the words in *der Apfel* | |
| ŋ  as *ng* in *song* | ʃ  as *sh* |
| ɫ  as *el* in *label* | ʒ  as *s* in *leisure* |
| θ  as *th* in *thin* | ɥ  as *u* in French *nuit* |
| ð  as *th* in *this* | |

Fig. 4. A guide to the values of I.P.A. symbols as used in this book.

the sound represented by 'r' (say in 'story') may vary to an extreme degree, rolled, flapped, labialised to an extent that produces a sound more like 'w'. And yet these various sounds are recognised as belonging to the class 'r'. Such variants are possible as long as no confusion between words or sentences arises as a result of confusion with another sound group. Not only do individual variations operate at each sound, the other sounds also have their influence. This context of sound results in considerable acoustic variation. The 't' of 'tin' /tin/ is different from the 't' of 'tuck' /tʌk/ or my 't' in 'tin' is different from the sound you make in that word. Let us be precise about these two 't' sounds, calling the 't' of 'tin' t¹ and the 't' of 'tuck' t². Now suppose John Brown uses t¹ (the body of the tongue pushed up and forward) in 'tuck' and t² (the body of the tongue drawn down and back) in 'tin' (thus changing round what are, strictly speaking, two distinct sounds). No linguistic change occurs since English is organised in such a way that the difference is *not* contrastive. But if the vocal chords were brought into vibration instead, the substitution of voiced t¹ and t² for voiceless t¹ and t² would produce 'din' and 'duck'. Whereas two variants in one direction (tongue position) are felt as non-contrastive, variants in another direction (voice) are contrastive in English. If we call t¹ /ʈ/ and t² /t/ another language might contrast tongue position and /ʈin/ would mean something completely different from /tin/, while the alternation of voice and voicelessness in /tʌk/, /dʌk/ might be merely an individual idiosyncrasy—a feature at the level of idiolect.

Variations between cardinal points on consonant and vowel 'maps' may clearly become contrastive in different languages. Differences of length and stress may also acquire significance in different languages. The contrast of /bid/ and /biːd/ may be insignificant in another language. It is unlikely that there would be confusion between 'convict (noun) and con'vict (verb) (because of grammatical signals which will be discussed below), nevertheless stress can clearly be contrastive.

Related sounds may be grouped into one *phoneme* when they never contrast within the language. The sounds represented by 'r' in 'rim' and 'ram' are different only because of the phonic context and within the linguistic system of each individual. All the variants of 'r' are *allophones* of the phoneme /r/ just as the variant pronunciations of 't' were allophones of the one phoneme /t/ in English because they are felt by users of that system to be merely different exponents of the same 'sound'. Minimal contrasts between words offer a practical test but are not the only indication of a phoneme.

It may sometimes be necessary to represent individual or regional allophonic variations very exactly, and then a fine phonetic transcription can be used, employing a vast array of symbols to specify these minimal allophonic variations. Such fine transcriptions are usually shown between square brackets [ ]. For most practical purposes, however, transcription at the level of *langage*, using broad phonemic transcription, is sufficient. Within a language, what matters for most purposes is that the meaningful contrasts should be shown, and these, as we have seen, are the phonemes of each language. Allophones, which may be shown in narrow transcription, are variations conditioned by context but without significant contrast. For example, /d/ after the front vowel /i/ ('Sid') will, in English, be pronounced by most speakers with a tongue position slightly more forward in the mouth than with the /d/ after the back vowel /ʌ/ ('sud') but this has no significance. Allophonic variations are therefore not shown in general writings about language. Any move away from phonemic transcription, of course, opens a scale of almost infinite delicacy of representation. Transcription can be refined to the point where it becomes useless, unless a description of the individual speaker or group of speakers is appended.

Below are given three transcriptions of the sentence 'All of a sudden Sidney Carnaby came over faint'. The first is broad (phonemic) transcription:

/ɔːɫ əv ə sʌdn sidniː kaːnəbiː keim ouvə feint/

This is a representation of the categories of the phonic substance of this utterance. It makes no allowance for the variation within the phonemes symbolised. The second transcription takes account of these allophonic variants:

[ɔːɫ əv ə sʌdn̩ sidniː kaːnəbiː ḳeim ouvə feint]

The symbol ₊ shows an 'advanced' sound, i.e. one made more forward in the mouth than is the phoneme in isolation; the mark ˌ under a consonant indicates syllabicity. This degree of refinement in notation can be useful as an instrument in language teaching. Indeed phonetic transcription has, of necessity, played a major part in teaching non-European languages.

The phonetic description of newly discovered languages will always work with precise notation of individual speech. Phonemic grouping and the description of normal allophonic variation is the result of the amalgamation of numerous speech acts as noted. Such notation is inevitably much finer than this example. It is intended as a possible fine notation of the pronunciation by an individual of the sentence given as illustration above

[ɔˑɫ v ə sʌdn̩ sidni kʰaˑnəbi ḳʰeim oɞvə feinʔ]

The vowels have generally been shortened; i and ɞ are shorter respectively than iː and u. The symbol ˑ shows that vowel length is shorter than usual, but the vowel is not short; ʰ shows that there is aspiration in the individual's production of this sound.

Variations of *stress* and *tone* (voice pitch) also form part of the system of organised sound (the *phonology* of the language). There has been mention already of one of the formal functions of stress in English in distinguishing between noun and verb /ˈpəːmit/ and /pəˈmit/. In another case, 'export', the verb may be stressed on the first syllable /wiː ˈikspɔːt tuː litł/ or the second /wiː iksˈpɔːt tuː litł/. The difference here has significance, if any, only at the level of *parole*, telling something of the stylistic variations of any individual's speech.

In some languages stress always occurs in the same position in words, in others there is no consistency. Some languages use stress as a distinctive mark in their phonological system at word level. In others stress contrasts sentences.

> He knows ˈsomething about it
> He ˈknows something about it
> ˈHe knows something about it
> He knows something aˈbout it

are contrasted partly by stress. Of course,

> He knows something about ˈit

would be impossible unless *it* were taken to be a full lexical item (i.e. noun), as 'it' was used by film publicists at one time as a synonym for 'glamour'.

Tone (voice pitch) may operate in some languages at word level, in others at not less than sentence level. In Chinese and other tone languages the four, five or more tones are the only distinguishing feature between groups of otherwise homophonic items. The speaker of languages such as English, where item-contrasts are made by variations in the interplay of vocal organs, finds particular difficulty where similarly delicate distinctions produced by a vastly different system, e.g. voice pitch, feature so prominently. Clearly, very precise training in the discrimination and production of such tone variation is an essential preliminary to the learning of such languages.

At the phrase or sentence level sequences of pitch, called *intonation*, offer linguistic contrasts—where such sequences are not predetermined by the tones featured by words in the language. It is not possible here to do more than remind the reader that there are intonational differences. A common system of marking is used in the places where reference is made by example to this phenomenon of pronunciation. In these cases the reader will have to infer the possible value of the marking from the stated 'meaning'. There is clearly a contrastive difference in the contexts appropriate to the following two intonational patterns:

> I was expecting them to call
> /ai wəz əksˈpɛktiŋ ðəm təˌkɔːl/

where the expectation was high (and they probably have called)

> /⁻ai wəz əksˌˌpɛktiŋ ðəm tə ˈkɔːl/

where there is disappointment that they have not called.

In a tonal language such variation in tune would have significance at the level of the word rather than, as in English, at the level of the total sentence. The sum of contrasts at word level would produce a difference much greater than the contrast between sequences. The contrasts presented by intonational patterns in English are not much less complicated for the foreign learner to understand. Whereas the learner of a tonal language can consult a dictionary in which the tones are specified, no-one has yet produced a full dictionary of *sentence* meanings differentiated by a wide range of intonational possibilities.

So far the phonological features we have looked at have been positive, although deriving their significance by contrast and therefore from the absence of all the other possibilities. Phonological description includes the study of *junctures*, significant breaks in the stream of speech. At word- and phrase-level, juncture can contrast items such as 'an ocean' and 'a notion'. At higher levels its significance is not always easy to specify. Its presence (marked with +) in sentences like:

> The Frenchman who came to see us has returned to France
> /ðə frɛntʃmən hu keim tə siː əs həz ritəːnd tə fraːns/

> the Frenchman, who came to see us, has returned to France
> /ðə frɛntʃmən + hu keim tə siː əs + həz ritəːnd tə fraːns/

is well known, and is marked in graphic substance by a comma.

There have been attempts to extend the phonemic theory to stress, intonation and juncture but no consistent theory has yet been produced to compare with the phoneme in its *segmental* rôle amongst vowels and consonants. Prosodic analysis, too, which attempts to apply a unified analysis to all these features remains to be fully developed.

Consideration of the segmental and suprasegmental features of language have dealt with linguistic features of speech. In all the components of phonology: vowel or consonant (segmental), stress, tone or intonation, and juncture (suprasegmental), significance has derived from the system, from the contrasts between all the possibilities within that feature. Graphology presents nothing like this variety, although the significance of the shapes derives, similarly, from contrast with the other possibilities; 'n' is not 'm' because of a minimal difference in construction; 'ram' is different from 'ran' for the same reason. On this basis some linguists have proposed a graphemic analysis of written language. Such minimal contrasts are of value for learners whose native language uses a different script, and they suggest ways in which learning could be eased as with work in pronunciation of the language. Russian '*n*' /p/ contrasts with '*н*' /n/, '*g*' /d/ with '*г*' /g/.

The difference between the spoken and written forms of a language is as great as that between their representative substances. The difference has as yet scarcely been realised. It has generally been assumed that the static quality of the written language is characteristic of language generally and that any other forms are necessarily 'sub-standard'. The linguist has no place in this argument. His job is merely to record what is happening, to suggest the possibilities of either medium. The teacher has a duty in this respect. He should recognise the existence of two forms of language which serve different purposes and use different techniques.

'Suddenly Sidney Carnaby felt faint' would be a probable written version of the spoken language sentence given earlier in a number of transcriptions. The difference, in practice, would be wider, particularly in a much larger context. Consider the speech of an educated native speaker of English.

There he was, that Sidney Carnaby, who never used to touch a drop, knocking back pints at a time; no wonder all of a sudden he came over faint. Can't wonder at it, the rate he was going.

How would he write about the event?

Sidney Carnaby, who would drink no alcohol at one time, was consuming considerable quantities of beer. As a result of the amount he had drunk, of course, he began to feel faint.

No comparison of quality is possible here. As a formulation of English neither is particularly good or particularly bad. The only possibility of comparison is on their respective relevance to the purpose of the description. Any such assessment must include the use to which they will be put. If the aim is an artistic production the texture of the spoken language must be weighed against the texture of the written language. Clearly, less control can be exercised over the presentation of the former. On the other hand, the competent use of the spoken language is more effective in many circumstances than is the written language, but the necessary ability is rare. In fact my 'spoken language' example is far more organised than most would be in practice. Even so, the linguistic differences are considerable. Phonemic transcription of the 'spoken' version will show one or two phonological features hidden by the graphic substance.

/'ðɛə hiː‚wɔz + 'ðæt 'sidniː ‚kaːnəbiː huː 'nɛvə 'juːst tə 'tʌtʃ ə
That night          Sidney Carnaby, who would drink no alcohol
‚drɔp + nɔkiŋ bæk 'paints ət ə‚ taim + nou ‚wʌndə + ‚ɔːl əv ə
at one time, was consuming considerable quantities of beer. As a
‚sʌdən + hiː ‚keim ouvə ᵛfeint + kaːnt ᵛwʌndər ‚æt it + ðə ‚reit ᵛhiː
result of the amount he had drunk, of course, he began to feel
wəz ‚gouwiŋ/
faint.

Ignoring the differences in substance, there are many differences such as (spoken) clause/(written) vocabulary items (there he was/ that night); constructed (phrasal) verbs/lexical items (knocking back/consuming); repetitive emotive vocabulary/logical structure (no wonder, can't wonder/as a result) which a full analysis would show.

    We have considered the selection and organisation of sounds in the phonological system of language. The three remaining levels of analysis, at which most linguistic descriptions operate, are *morphology*, *syntax* and *lexis*. Language is a continuum, an unbroken flow, and it is misleading to suggest that these levels are separate entities. The four levels, with phonology or graphology, are interwoven in a highly complex manner. The functional relationships of morphology, syntax and lexis are the concern of modern linguistic theories, as we shall see. Theories of the relationship between phonology or graphology and grammar are little developed as yet. At least one of the major theories of general linguistic analysis will eventually pursue the morphographemic and morphophonemic descriptions as far as the phenomena will allow.

    Morphology is concerned with the changing shape of words in their different relations with other words. The term 'word', like the term 'sentence' which we shall be dealing with later, is a working concept which can only be defined *functionally* in terms of the language being studied. No satisfactory definition of either term has been produced which would have application to all languages. Such definition is not in fact essential since, like certain undefined terms in other disciplines, the concepts are used only as a starting-point. In English and all other European languages the word is marked by a space before and after it in graphology, by the possibility of its isolation and by certain contrasts of stress pattern in the phonology. Even so, these simple criteria are sometimes mutually exclusive. The criteria do suggest that 'blackbird' /'blækbəːd/ is one word and 'black bird' /blæk'bəːd/ two, but it works less smoothly for 'White House' /'hwait haus/ and 'White house' /hwait 'haus/.

Morphology is interested in the contrasts between forms like:

**A** bird goat sheep mouse duck      horse child
**B** birds goats sheep mice    duck, ducks horses children

These words are clearly related vertically, as a small paradigm in each case. Their horizontal relationship is derived from their syntactical function. All the forms shown in line A have been found before 'is' (or ''s') in the graphic substance of English, before /iz/ or /s/ or /z/ in the phonic substance; all the forms in line B have been found, respectively, before 'are' or ''re' and /aː/ or /ə/. If native English speakers make the formal change as implied between lines A and B consistently in context with formal change in other words we are clearly dealing with two classes of word, class A and class B.

We can control class A and class B in context:

A The bird is singing/ or The bird's singing
B The birds are singing/ or The birds're singing

The graphological contrast between A and B is: 'is'/'are' (*or* 's/'re). Phonemically the sentences are:

A /ðə bəːd iz siŋiŋ/ or /ðə bəːdz siŋiŋ/
B /ðə bəːdz aː siŋiŋ/ or /ðə bəːdz ə siŋiŋ/

The phonological contrast between A and B is /iz/ /aː/ (or /z/ /zə/).

From an analysis of a number of the items and their formal changes in a phonological context a descriptive linguist might say that a frequent change in speech was merely the addition of the neutral vowel /ə/. Compare A /ðə bouts rɛdiː/ 'the boat's ready' and B /ðə bouts ə rɛdiː/ 'the boats are ready'. However, this rule does not apply throughout the language and not in very different contexts. Compare A /ðə maus laiks tʃiːz/ 'the mouse likes cheese' and B /ðə mais laik tʃiːz/ 'the mice like cheese'. The interchange /laiks/laik/ remains whatever item from class A and B is selected for this context.

The relationship of class A and class B may be characterised as that of 'singular' to 'plural' but only because a deduction as to number has been made for each member by reference to a situation. They have, nevertheless, been distinguished *formally* before any statement has been made about meaning.

It is important to make this point, for one of the grave weaknesses of traditional grammar has been its primary concern with naming linguistic items and deducing their function from these names. Modern linguistic theories are concerned solely with *formal* relationships. Many linguists, indeed, would reject the study of meaning (semantics) as having no place in general linguistics. This will be of interest in dealing with *lexis* but for the moment we are concerned with a formal analysis. The names we give to the classes when they have been established are often drawn from the terms of traditional grammar, but the classes are *not* defined by those names. The temporary nature of such names is clear. A linguist may call class A 'singular' but he is likely to call those forms which contrast, here class B, 'non-singular'. 'Duck' is in class A (let's class it 'singular') because it is usually associated with certain forms of other words and it shares this consistent association (*collocation*) with other words we have grouped in class A:

> The goat looks sad
> The duck looks sad

Against this we have the forms in class B and their formal collocations:

> The goats look sad
> The ducks look sad

But 'duck' is in class B too because it sometimes behaves formally like 'ducks':

but not
> The duck breed young (in those parts of Europe)
>
> The goat breed young (in those parts of Europe)

It is quite possible to distinguish between class B 'duck' and 'ducks' by specifying the kinds of verb, etc., with which they may each collocate. Both, however, are 'non-singular', neither being 'more class B' than the other.

If we look at items which belong to class B in English we find that many of them are characterised graphologically by final 's'. Examples of words of which this is not true have been included deliberately in the paradigm above, but the overwhelming majority of English nouns have written forms which vary by adding final 's'. Phonologically the variation is more complex. The final sound may be /z/ (as in 'bird*s*'), /s/ (as in 'goat*s*'), /iz/ or /əz/ (as in 'horse*s*'). These changes are regular, being conditioned by the phonetic context (/z/ after a voiced sound (as /d/), /s/ after unvoiced consonant (as /t/), /iz/ after /s/ or /z/). Each is the smallest unit of formal change (*morpheme*). They all perform the same formal function (here the change from class A to class B collocations). In this respect they bear a similarity to the allophones which are the smallest unit of phonic change. Like allophones, it may be said that morphemes are merely aspects of a class of minimal unit. The graphological 's' on the one hand and the phonological /z, s, iz/ on the other may be said to belong to a morpheme group which characterises some members of group B in English, in other words a morpheme of plurality. The term *allomorph* would then be given to these exponents of the morpheme group. To have validity, the concept of allomorph must presumably apply to all variations dominated by the same type of formal collocation. The formal change from class A to class B is not always by the addition of morphemes /s, z, iz/. A thoroughgoing allomorphic analysis will postulate *zeromorphs* (that is, analytic units without overt expression) for changes of the type 'The *sheep* looks sad/The *sheep* look sad'. The concept of zero in extending the applicability of an analysis is accepted by most linguists.

Further allomorphic analysis of 'plurality' in English must deal with such changes as 'mouse'/'mice' and 'child'/'children'. Various theories have been suggested to deal with this kind of inconsistency. Vowel change may be regarded as an allomorph (i.e. as in mouse/mice); 'ren' may be considered as another; if 'en' is taken as an allomorph, as the pattern of 'ox/oxen', 'childr-' may be regarded as a root form of plurality.

The relentless extension of the morphemic/allomorphic analysis of language is valid in a full-scale description, but for most practical purposes a morphemic analysis, with some grouping of allomorphs will be sufficient.

To return to our earlier consideration of the morpheme. *Morpho-phonology* (or *morphonology*) has suggested a morphemic group of plurality /s, z, iz/. In the teaching of German, of course, such classification of the formal characteristics of plurality is well known (e.g. Frau (+en), Sub-class: Wand (+vowel change+e> Wände)).

Words are composed of these minimal units of form. Some morphemes (*bound*) can only be used in conjunction with others, others (*free*) can exist on their own. In 'unpredictable' a morphological analysis would produce

| | |
|---|---|
| 'un-': | a bound morpheme |
| 'predict': | a free morpheme |
| '-able': | a bound morpheme |

An allomorphic analysis would in this case go on to suggest that 'un-' belonged to the same morpheme class as 'in-', 'non-', 'a-'; '-able' would belong to the same group as '-ible' (phonemically they are often the same -/əbl̩/). In this example the free morpheme may also be termed the '*root morpheme*' since it is the morpheme left when the affixes 'un-' and '-able' have been taken away. A root morpheme may be bound or free, an affix is always bound.

Important morphological changes in English, apart from word-formation, occur in verbal forms 'likes'/'like', 'like'/'liked'. Many words at present treated as vocabulary are seen differently in a morphophonological analysis. The contrast between *declarative* sentence and *interrogative* sentence is phonemically as follows:

/ai laik kæts/
/ai dount laik kæts/

between the *emphatic* and interrogative:

/ai du: laik kæts/
/ai dount laik kæts/

The contrasts here are clearly of a different quality from the following:

/ai nɛvə laik kæts/
/ai laik siŋiŋ/
/ai sə:tənli: laik kæts/

There is good reason for considering items like /du:/ and /dʌznt/ and /didnt/ as morphemic units in the same way that /t/ is considered in, say, /ai laikt kæts/ as a 'past' (or 'non-present') morpheme. In the same way the contrasts between some of the hypothetical forms in English are phonemically as follows:

/if hi: kɔ:lz ʃi:l tɛl him/
/if hi kɔ:ld ʃi:d tɛl him/
/if hi:d kɔ:ld ʃi:d əv told him/

If we characterise these complete structures as, respectively,
'possible', 'improbable', 'highly improbable' (rather than by constructing them from so-called 'tense' paradigms) we can set up
formal patterns such as:

| x | x | xZ | xL | x | x: | 'possible' |
| x | x | xD | xD | x | x: | 'improbable' |
| x | xD | xD | xD | əv past x: | | 'highly improbable' |

Where x indicates a consistent item, capitals indicate a morphophonemic unit, and 'past' is a notation for a consistent relationship
the forms of which can be obtained from a transliteration of x at
that point and a reference to the morphographemic or morphophonemic list which can be provided (i.e. looking up one possible
exponent of x at this point ('tell') we find the past form 'told').
Emphasis has been placed on the establishment of formal categories
and on the importance of *formal* contexts and these are also the
basis of work on syntax. Moreover, the establishment of these categories and functional descriptions has been based on contrasts.

Language is a system, and within this system the rôle of contrast
is central. There is no universal system which is yet known to be
true of all languages, indeed no two languages are structured in the
same way. The formal categories of one language may parallel those
of another language paradigmatically (i.e. vertically), the syntactical
operation of these categories within these languages will be different
and so will the system of contrasts with any other language.

The past (or 'non-present') verb forms in English contrast with
the present verb forms syntactically; French past verb forms contrast with French present verb forms. There is no cross-reference
between these two languages outside a comparison of the *whole*
formal system of both. Within this contrastive system, unique to
each language, there are further contrastive systems.

In describing the categories through whose contrasts the systems
of a language function, symbols become important, since they
allow the analysis to be seen to have a wider truth that might
otherwise be hidden by the complexities of morphophonemic and
morphographemic relationships. The naming of parts of speech
attempted the same thing but inevitably, by working paradigmatically only, prejudged formal (syntactical) relationships in terms
of the linguistic structure (Latin or Greek) from which they had
been culled. Moreover, once linguistic items have been named, they
begin to behave in accordance with the names, such is the magic of
language! An 'adjective' is 'attributive' or 'predicative'. If, like

'enough' (e.g. 'enough is enough') it only appears in a predicative position it is presumably 'defective'—or perhaps it is a defective adverb. On the other hand, I may be content to say that there is a common formal relationship which may be described as: Subject + BE + $adj_x$. I have created an *ad hoc* category which is formally true if I define the symbols to mean 'any word which may precede and collocate with any part of the paradigms of the verb BE may be followed by any word which I shall list as belonging to category $adj_x$'. This description is more precise than any naming would be, and is truer of English, because it uses the forms of that language. Whereas 'adjective' could only have meaning if I described it as 'modifying' or 'qualifying' another sort of word. Instead I have categorised a particular word in formal terms. The symbols used will have value as long as my analysis is valid. They will have added advantage if they are a reminder of an important morphological feature. Thus a basic French structure is:

$$\text{Subj.} + \text{aux.} + \text{V} + \text{é}$$
$$\text{J(e)} + \text{ai} + \text{pay} + \text{é}$$

If my analysis is accurate, moreover, each symbol will be precise enough to refer to a practical list of exponents (words and morphemes) which can be drawn up.

Syntax, as we have seen, deals with horizontal relationship of words in use. It is impossible to deal with morphology and syntax separately, for they are complementary.

'The woman threw the ball' is only reversible in English if there is a corresponding reversal of the relationships and therefore the meaning:

The ball threw the woman

Similarly in French 'La femme a jeté la balle' is irreversible.

In German, however, morphology sometimes plays a more important part than syntax.

Den Ball warf die Frau

is possible, and the meaning is clear from the morphemic '-en' in association with Ball

Die Blume warf die Frau

is possible only with a special stress and intonational pattern, because there is no other formal contrast available.

| The woman | threw the ball |
|-----------|----------------|
| Who       | threw the ball? |
| We        | ate    a sandwich |

Whoever it
was who came
last week      took    those ashtrays

There are clearly syntactical classes illustrated here since the formal relationships are the same in each case and the changes are rung by straightforward substitution.

Parsing has traditionally been concerned with the *naming* of parts of speech. Moreover, any analysis has been unidirectional, left to right.

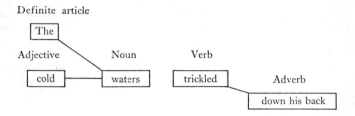

Such an analysis shows something about the sentence, but in an oversimplified form. It is nevertheless one kind of analysis of the *immediate constituents* of the stream of language which expounds this sentence. Like the word, the sentence defies definition. It is easily recognised in graphic substance by the upper case first letter and the full stop at the end. It is often marked in phonic substance by a certain intonational pattern or by a juncture. The nature of the sentence is precisely what most contemporary linguistic description endeavours to describe. No scientific analysis starts with a definition of what it is going to find at the end of the analysis. A definition of the sentence in a language would be a complete grammar of that language and further linguistic analysis would be superflous. Sentence may be taken to be coextensive with *utterance*. The latter may be thought of as that stream of sound which lies between two deliberate pauses and with a related intonation pattern. Sentence and utterance may for practical purposes be taken as synonymous in linguistic description, provided that they include both 'fire!' and 'no-one knows where he spent his last holiday and no-one ever will'.

There are certainly, in all languages, certain *basic sentence-types*, irreducible streams of language substance which serve as a basis for the (more numerous) longer sentences. One such basic sentence-type in English is:

Smith writes (noun + verb)

which can be expanded:

> Henry Smith writes letters home (noun phrase + verb phrase)
> Old Henry Smith writes letters daily (NP + VP)
> Noble old Henry Smith writes letters daily at 10.30 (NP + VP)

and so forth.

However long our resultant string of words, 'That noble old Henry Smith who liked mother so much...' can be substituted by 'Smith' (or by the symbol 'noun' or NP), and 'writes letter daily at 10.30 in that café opposite the cathedral...' by 'writes' (or by VP). No account has been taken of the meaning of the parts other than their formal interrelationship. If 'Smith' and 'writes' are said

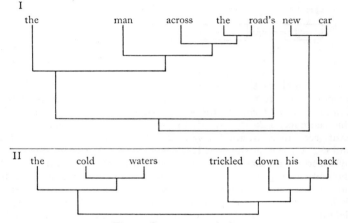

Fig. 5. Structure analysis.

to be the *head* words and the rest subordinate, this does not say anything about the meaning of the sentence. The most *important* word might be 'noble' or 'who liked mother so much' but this would only appear from analysis of the background and circumstances of its being produced—from its *context*.

An expansion of 'water trickled' to 'the cold waters trickled down his back' has the same *structure* as the sentence previously quoted, NP + VP.

There are also *non-favourite sentences*, such as exclamations, 'curses!', 'goodness gracious me!', and proverbial phrases, 'the more the merrier', which are not the basis for further normal expansions in the language (except by the poet or the comedian). A more interesting type of non-favourite sentence is the complement of a *favourite* (or basic) sentence. 'And where does Helen live now?' answer: basic sentence type: 'Has she moved then?' or: non-favourite sentence: 'The same place.' Non-favourite sentences of this kind are, of course, frequent in conversation but the despair of the language teacher who wants the pupil to respond with basic sentence type: 'Elle habite à Malmaison' rather than the (natural) non-favourite sentence 'A Malmaison'.

IC (immediate constituent) analysis is concerned with the inter-relationships of the components of a sentence. Opposite is the IC analysis of 'the cold waters trickled down his back'. It is obviously a clearer analysis of formal relationships than that shown on page 37. We see immediately the relationship between NP and VP. Within NP we can see the relationship of the article to the adj + noun; within VP the dominance of verb + adverb, and within the adverb the unity of possessive adjective + noun subordinate to the relationship of preposition and NP.

The groups shown by immediate constituent analysis as the components of the sentence may themselves be analysed further. In the nominal group 'the cold waters' the principal grammatical function is performed by 'waters'; the words 'the' and 'cold' are subordinate *grammatically* since we could replace the nominal group by 'waters' but not by the other words. The word performing the principal grammatical function is known as the *head-word* (or *head*). Such a description has *no* reference to meaning. This can be shown by a sentence like '*Dangerous animals* prowl the streets' where 'animals' is the head-word in the nominal group although 'dangerous' is obviously more important!

Analysis at morphemic level is possible but not common in IC description. Occasionally, however, it is the only level which will complete an analysis. In a complex English nominal group like '*the man across the road's* new car' such an analysis is essential.

Immediate constituent analysis deals with the completed utterance. It is not concerned with the structuring of the utterance but with its structure. In this respect it stands comparison with traditional grammatical analysis, except that it is concerned only with formal relationships which can be stated. It is therefore in tune with modern linguistic description. It is not, however, concerned with the formal *production* of streams of language.

The difference between IC analysis and a *transformational genera-*

*tive grammar* is that between a state and an activity. TGG (also called 'transformational grammar' for short) aims at establishing a set of descriptions of all the operations of language.

Each native speaker of a language is equipped with an intuitive 'internal grammar' (cf. langue) which he uses in producing or understanding sentences. This 'grammar' enables him to produce and understand sentences, moreover, which he has *never* produced or heard before. It enables him to recognise sentences as 'well-formed' or grammatical, as semi-grammatical or as non-grammatical. In this an educated speaker may refer consciously to the precepts and proscriptions of his teachers, of prescriptive grammar books, or of national academies, but his basic decision about the acceptability or otherwise of sentences, which is apparently instinctive, will often be outside these limitations. The 'naïve' speaker of the language, moreover, will be able to make a similar assessment just as decidedly, without any training in grammar or any acquaintance with 'authorities'.

Part of this 'internal grammar' may be the expansion of basic sentence-types and substitution of items within these expanded sentences. But it is certain that many sentences in a language cannot simply be expansions of this kind. This can be shown by two pairs of English sentences that have featured frequently in writings on TGG. The first pair is:

> John is easy to please
> John is eager to please

On the surface these have the same structure, but they are obviously different. This can be shown by changing them from active to passive voice (the asterisk is used to indicate a malformation of language which is being used as an illustration).

> John is easily pleased
> *John is eagerly pleased

The first sentence will transform to the passive voice, the second transformation is simply not possible. Again the structure of

and

> I expected the doctor *to examine John*
>
> I persuaded the doctor *to examine John*

are the same. Transformation to the passive voice, however, shows a different structure:

> I expected *John to be examined by the doctor*
> ('I expected John' is a completely different sentence)

and

> I persuaded John *to be examined by the doctor*
> (' I persuaded John' is different only in the amount of detail included)

IC analysis of the original and resultant structures would show this difference *but would not account for the change*. TGG endeavours to describe the operation which relates such pairs and therefore sets out to account for any structure operationally. In so doing TGG does not attempt to re-create the native speaker's 'intuition'. It does not pretend to follow the same path from sentence A to sentence B as the native speaker: it does attempt to describe the most reliable and most efficient path. The aim of TGG is to establish a grammar which will produce and recognise in any one language well-formed sentences and no other sentences.

Transformational grammar consists of two sets of syntactical rules: *phrase structure rules* and *transformational rules*. Phrase structure rules describe the expansion of certain basic sentence types until an actual sentence is produced ('terminal string'). Underlying a certain number of sentences (basic sentence types) in any language are *kernel* structures from which they can be derived by a number of phrase-structure rules. As can be seen, the kernel sentence merely expounds an underlying structure. Many linguists prefer to talk about the *initial string* (represented always by S). Stages between initial and terminal strings are known as *intermediate strings*.

A set of phrase structure rules could look like this:

$S \rightarrow Nom + VP$  ('Sentence (or initial string) may be rewritten as...')

$VP \rightarrow (Prev) \ Aux + MV$  ('VP may be rewritten as: preverbal adverb [i.e. those adverbs listed as preverbal] + auxiliary + main verb')

$Aux \rightarrow Tn \ (Modal) \ (have + en) \ (be + ing)$  ('Aux may be rewritten as a tense morpheme + (perhaps) a modal verb + perhaps) (have + en) or (be + ing)')

$MV \rightarrow \begin{Bmatrix} be + pred \\ V \end{Bmatrix}$  ('MV may be rewritten as be + pred. (further defined) *or* verb (further defined)')

$Nom \rightarrow \begin{Bmatrix} PRO_D + PRO_N \\ Det + N + N^o \end{Bmatrix} + (S)$  ('Nom may be rewritten as

> one
> some + body *or* a determiner
> thing

(*Det* can be further defined and components selected from dictionary lists) + a noun + a number morpheme')

+ (S) in the last rewrite rule given here means that an additional terminal string may be derived. Since this choice occurs in the re-writing of every *Nom* there is a possibility of an infinite number of sentences in the terminal string. The element of *recursiveness* accounts for such sentences as:

He may have been singing *and dancing*.
He may have been singing and then found that he had lost his voice, which was no bad thing...

The phrase-structure rules given here have been only a small part of those available but would already account for a large number of terminal strings. It is very easy to understand the symbols, and this

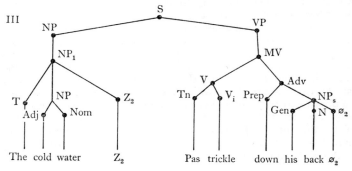

Fig. 6. Deep structure.

would reduce the *apparent* complexity of the rules stated here. In reality they describe very succinctly the structure of a number of English sentence-types. We might select as terminal string

$$Det + N + N^0 + Tn + Modal + (have + en) + V_t + det + N + N^0$$

($V_t + det + N + N^0$ comes from an expansion of V). If we then select from the lexicon of English lexical items listed against each symbol we could produce

$$The + strong + wind + Z_2 + Pas + may + (have + en) + demolish + that + old + house + ø_2$$

($Z_2$ and $ø_2$ are symbols for respectively the morpheme of plurality and the morpheme of singularity in nominal groups.) The resulting sentence is:

The strong winds may have demolished that old house.

The interrelationships may be seen more clearly in diagrammatic form. The diagram of the derivation of a string from phrase-structure rules takes the form of a branching tree. They are sometimes called *phrase-structure* markers or *p-markers*.

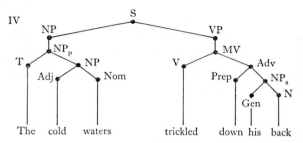

Fig. 7. Surface structure.

It will be seen that the P-marker of surface-structure analyses the word level, and the diagram is similar to that produced by IC analysis. The dots in the tree diagram are called *nodes*, and the higher nodes are said to *dominate* those lower in the tree. Thus 'VP dominates MV'. The deep structure analysis is carried down to morphemic level.

If we apply the morphographemic rules of the language the teminal string derived on page 42 may be rewritten:

The + strong + winds + might + have + demolished + that + old + house.

In the next stage the plus signs are removed. The passive voice transformation of this sentence may be effected by introducing the passive morpheme (by + Psv) into the phrase-structure rules. The conditions for the introduction of this morpheme can be defined (presence of $V_t$ (i.e. transitive verb), etc.)

$$Nom_1 + pas + modal + have + en + V_t$$
The + strong + winds +      might + have + en + demolish
+ by + Psv + $Nom_2$
+ by + psv + that + old + house

Transformational rule 1 (⇒ is the sign of the application of a transformational rule)

$$Nom + Pas + modal + have + en + V_t + by + Psv + Nom_2 \Rightarrow$$
$$+ Pas + modal + have + en + V_t + by + Nom_1 + Nom_2$$

Transformational rule 2

$+\text{Pas}+\text{modal}+\text{have}+\text{en}+V_t+\text{by}+\text{Nom}_1+\text{Nom}_2 \Rightarrow$
$\qquad \text{Nom}_2+\text{Pas}+\text{modal}+\text{have}+\text{en}+V_t+\text{by}+\text{Nom}_1$

Transformational rule 3

$\text{Nom}_2+\text{Pas}+\text{modal}+\text{have}+\text{en}+V_t+\text{by}+\text{Nom}_1 \Rightarrow$
$\qquad \text{Nom}_2+\text{Pas}+\text{modal}+\text{have}+\text{en}+\text{be}+\text{en}+V_t+\text{by}+\text{Nom}_1$

(in certain cases Affix + verb $\Rightarrow$ Verb + affix)

Another transformational rule that I have already used without acknowledgement allows us to rewrite this as: $\text{Nom}_2+\text{modal}+\text{Pas}+\text{have}+\text{be}+\text{en}+V_t+\text{en}+\text{by}+\text{Nom}_1$. Application of the appropriate morphographemic rules (as well as instatement of items from the lexicon) produces:

That + old + house + might +      have + been + demolished
$\text{Nom}_2 +$              modal + Pas + have + been + $V_t$ + en +

by + $\text{Nom}_1$
by the strong winds

An earlier illustration of deep ambiguity was, it will be remembered:

1. John is easy to please
2. John is eager to please

Sentence 1 might have this derivation:

$NP_1 +$ be + $\text{adj}_y$ + PRO +     $V_t$ +      $NP_1$ $\Rightarrow$
John + is +  easy + someone + pleases + John $\Rightarrow$

$NP_1 +$ be + $\text{adj}_y$ + $\text{Nom}_{\text{infin}\,v}$
John + is +  easy + (to + please)

where $\text{Nom}_{\text{infin}\,v}$ represents the infinitive associated with $V_t$. Sentence 2, on the other hand, might have this derivation:

$NP_1 +$ be + $\text{adj}_y$ + $NP_n$ + $V_t$ +      PRO    $\Rightarrow$
John + is +  eager + John + pleases + someone $\Rightarrow$

$NP_1 +$ be + $\text{adj}_y$ + $\text{Nom}_{\text{infin}\,v}$
John + is +  eager + (to + please)

The native speaker's ability to discriminate in cases of ambiguity such as 'John's ready to pay', 'John's there to see' may rest on a parallel kind of operation.

The analyses have been concerned with the ordering of units of language in strings, and with the nature of morphological and syntactical relationships. Only in considering root morphemes has the study come near to dealing with lexical items. Admittedly, transformations lead eventually to selection of items to clothe the symbolised relationships, but the very use of symbols results from an attempt to treat of formal relationships alone.

Another major theory of linguistic description has formalised concepts of *scale and category* to deal with the analysis of language. Unlike transformational generative grammar, scale and category grammar is concerned less with the operational aspects of language than with the structuring of forms. In many ways scale and category grammar compares with a thoroughgoing version of the phrase-structure part of the transformational-generative analysis.

The *categories* of scale and category grammar consist of *system*, *class*, *structure* and *unit*. The *system* referred to is that found in all modern descriptions of language. As we have seen already (page 32), formal components of language have significance only on the basis of their membership of a system. Descriptive linguistics works for much of the time by substituting *units* of language and thereby assigning these units to *classes*. We may divide the units of English into the following classes: sentence, clause, group, word and morpheme. This in itself presents a system, ranging from the sentence, which functions in situations, to the morpheme, which is, by definition, the smallest unit of grammar. Each class has a certain *structure*. The sentence, for instance, may consist of elements such as subject (S), verb (or predicator) (P) and complement (C) or adjunct (A) and have a structure which can be expressed SPA or SPC or SPCA, etc. However the elements vary in sequence, the declaratory sentence in English must always order S before P and P before C. This can be expressed $\overrightarrow{SPCA}$. This sequence is obligatory but may be discontinuous, $\overset{-}{S}A\overrightarrow{PC}$.

The *scales* of this grammar are: *rank*, *exponence* and *delicacy*. There is a range of classes which is shown in the P-marker diagrams of transformational-generative grammar and in the diagrams of IC analysis. In both these types of diagram a hierarchy is clearly visible, indeed nodes higher in the P-marker are said to 'dominate' those lower down. In the scale and category grammar of English the hierarchy is: sentence, clause, group (or 'phrase'), word and morpheme. The sentence consists of one or more clauses; the clause of one or more groups and so on. It is on this question in scale and category grammar of a fixed *hier*archy of *rank* which operates, for syntax, only downwards that there is most disagreement between linguists.

A concept which scale and category description has introduced is that of *rankshift*. 'Cambridge is a delightful old town' is a sentence which is composed of one clause. In 'That Cambridge is a delightful old town presents many town planning problems' the clause has taken its place at S in a sentence composed of one clause with structure SPC. The clause has undergone rankshift since it could be replaced by a noun ('Cambridge') which would be representing a *group*, and a group is lower in the descriptive hierarchy than a clause. Further degrees of rankshift are possible, as in 'That Cambridge is a delightful old town, offering visual delights to the student and the visitor, presents...'. A non-finite clause ('...offering visual delights to the student and the visitor...') (structure PCA) has undergone rankshift to function at Q (let us say 'as an adjective') to the rankshifted clause ('That Cambridge is a delightful old town...') functioning as nominal group.

All modern linguistic descriptions work with notions, that is at a level where language is a system or set of all the possibilities and is not yet clothed in the *substance* of scratches or sounds. SPCA indicates the structure of a typical English sentence more clearly than, say, 'My sister likes strawberries with apricot jam'. Moreover, it allows *all* the lexical possibilities of English within the elements and sequence indicated.

The scale of exponence deals with the relationship of form to expression. As we have seen earlier, this language code uses sounds and scratches selected from the enormous range of all possible sounds and scratches available. The *interlevel* between phonetics (which deals with all the possible range of articulate human sounds) and the structure of language is *phonology*; that between graphics and structure *graphology* (or 'orthography').

Clothing the sentence-structure SPA in a selection of scratches we have:

(S) That old house (P) might have been demolished (A) by the strong winds

At the same time this sentence consists of one clause, having (in this case) exponents identical with those of the sentence. The clause consists of three groups: a nominal group (functioning at S), a verbal group (functioning at P) and an adverbial group (functioning at A, the '*adjunct*' of the structure of this particular sentence).

Each group consists of a number of words. The nominal group (at S), for example, has the structure: M (for 'modifier', i.e. that which precedes the headword in the group), H (for 'headword'). A typical structure of the nominal group in English in MHQ, e.g.

M    H       Q<br>big/houses/in the town

(Q for 'qualifier', i.e. that which follows the headword in the group), where there is no limit to the number of exponents at M and Q.

Our analysis of the structure of this sentence has been at surface level or the level of *primary delicacy*. This concept of delicacy is much debated. As part of scale and category grammar it is described as a *cline*, that is as a continuum in which there is no real separation of the stages. Many linguists, however, maintain that there can only be one degree of delicacy in the classification of the elements of structure; indeed that descriptive grammar must aim at accounting for *all* events in the language; it can do nothing less.

The nominal group of the sentence type expounded in print above has a primary structure MMH, expounded by 'that old house'. We cannot expound the structure as 'old that house', so there must be a distinction between the two elements M. In scale and category grammar these are symbolised (at *secondary delicacy*) by deictic (D, e.g. demonstrative adjectives and definite and indefinite articles) and adjective (E). The structure of the nominal group is now (at secondary level) DEH. Another nominal group representing this structure might be 'such an old house', DDEH. Since we cannot write 'a such old house (DDEH), the structure must be shown at a further degree of delicacy, at which $D_a D_b$ can be used to represent the sub-classes of D which contain, respectively, half//all//both $(D_a)$ and a(an)//$\Theta$//the//some $(D_b)$. ($\Theta$ is the sign for zero.) There are clearly further degrees of delicacy within these sub-classes, in the direction of a degree of delicacy which will account for all the language.

The formulation of the scale and category grammar envisages the attainment of greater degrees of delicacy until all items are included in the description. However, delicacy of description falls short of the total analysis.

The structure of 'such an old house' is represented by $D_a D_b EH$. The same structure description represents 'half an old house', and $D_a$ represents 'both' in '*both* new houses', 'both extraordinary dwellings'. The formal analysis of these exponents of group structure can reach no greater degree of delicacy unless we can establish sub-classes for 'half' as against 'both', 'extraordinary' against 'new', 'houses' as against 'dwellings'.

At the point where delicacy ends, says scale and category grammar, *lexis* begins. The structure $D_a D_b EH$ is within a closed system, its exponents (which are, strictly, notional) are optional (being scratched out or articulated when the selection has been made). The options are in practice limited, since we can list all the possible exponents of certain sub-classes. The exponents of $D_b$, for example, are far less numerous than the exponents of E or H. To the latter classes we can add items freely; in the case of D sub-classes there is no such freedom. Here the concept of a *cline* is useful. There is no clear dividing line between grammar and lexis. Some language items ('*form words*') belong to completely open sets, in which the selection is bound by situational or collocational limitations only; other items ('structure words') belong to closed formal systems.

> (*a*) He was hit on the head ——— a tennis racket.
> (*b*) He was hit on the head with a ———.

These sentences are incomplete. In sentence (*a*) the missing word is a member of a closed system; it is to that extent redundant anyway. It is very probably '*with*'. If it is, then no matter if the radio does blare out and make it inaudible. It could be '*by*', in which case it simply must be audible. The missing word in sentence (*b*) is a member of an open set and is essential to this act of communication; it would only be redundant if we knew all the circumstances, if we already knew the situation. An analysis of situations could then bring even nouns into closed systems.

> (*c*) ——— a fine house.

From our knowledge of the sub-class operating at $D_a$ in this structure, we can select 'half', 'such', 'what' and nothing else. We can go no further with our formal analysis and yet we have a restricted choice. To the extent that we have a choice we can talk of a 'set' (and therefore 'lexis'), to the extent that our choice is largely restricted we can talk of a 'system' (and therefore grammar).

Any statement of structure such as $NP + Modal + V_t + NP$ or SPC can be realised in any way, (*a*) provided that lexical items are taken from the appropriate list in the lexicon (as transformational linguists would put it), or (*b*) provided that the association of items (*collocation*) is possible (as scale and category linguists would put it).

| S & C | S | P | | C |
|---|---|---|---|---|
| T G G | NP | + Modal | + $V_t$ | + NP |
| | the dog | may | see | the cat |
| | the cat | can | scratch | the dog |
| | 13 milkmen | should | finish | the job |

The last example is somewhat unusual, but is possible because milkmen/finish/job *do* collocate (shown in another part of the lexicon).

'A finger' collocates with 'bleed' but 'a page' can only collocate with 'bleed' in a printer's world (or, I suppose, in historical novels!).

'Put' collocates with 'children' and 'bed' but collocates with 'newspaper' and 'bed' only in the world of newspaper printing.

The possibilities of lexical collocation are quite wide. 'Play' and 'rifle' would not be a normal collocation, but members of an armed service have recently been seen on television 'playing rifles'! In normal language use, however, the possibilities are not exploited. Indeed, if this were not so the use and reception of language would be unbearable. *Redundancy* is high in the spoken language. 'Those mice like...' (Well?) I should have to underline with care the unusual collocation in 'Those mice like coffee', since my listener is not likely to perceive the non-redundant item unless I call his attention by saying 'Did you know—those mice—they like *coffee*'. Redundancy is based on both formal (i.e. grammatical) and lexical collocational probabilities.

Lexis offers an open set. New items can develop or be created without the meaning of existing items changing because of the additions. Grammar depends for its meaning on the closed system in which its formal relationships operate. The *form words* (nouns, verbs, adjectives and adverbs) contain the primary meaning of a sentence while the *structure words* (auxiliary verbs, prepositions and conjunctions) bind the form words in a meaningful sequence.

'It's plovish of Tilspot to gerint the quarls.' This is English, because the structure words are obviously English, although the new form words will have to be defined. If the morphemes were changed and the shape of the form words altered the Englishness would not be so obvious. 'It's plovuir of Estilsiporot to gerinl the quarloi.' On the other hand, the substitution of English form words and non-English structure words produces something quite non-English. 'Tir unpleasant bor Edward zul kill eth pigeons.' A more delightful example of this is to be found, of course, in 'Jabberwocky' in *Alice in Wonderland*.

Throughout linguistic description the principal descriptive tool is contrast. The collocation of lexical items is based on the comparative frequency of certain collocations in practical use and on the contrast in probability. In this way the 'meaning' of the lexical item is partly delimited. For the most part, however, its meaning is delimited by its contrast with near-synonyms and by the range of situations in which it may occur.

Traditionally the meaning of words has been the field of the philologist, the etymologist and the philosopher. Many linguists today would reject the contributions of these specialists. Indeed, as was probably necessary, 'meaning' and 'semantics' have played a comparatively small part in modern linguistic analysis, tainted as they were by a large component of unscientific or irrelevant analysis.

Modern linguists would prefer the thesaurus, which arranges words within the structured fields of reference of the language, to the dictionary, which attempts to define with words which are themselves defined with words, which...

On a much larger scale, collocation becomes the total linguistic context used within a certain situation. The term 'context of situation' was invented by Malinowski and first used extensively by J. R. Firth. The term may be taken to include such paralinguistic and supralinguistic events as sighs, gestures, grunts, actions. The analysis is obviously very difficult and the full definition of the 'contexts of situation' has yet to take place. Some analysis of paralinguistic features and of 'register' (variation in the selection of linguistic items for various purposes, including adjustment to different situations) is proceeding and some extension of this work can be expected. Such analysis of the situational use of language will concern itself with formal structures as much as with lexical items. 'He goes there every day' has a different 'meaning' from 'he's going there every day' (with reference to the present or non-past) but any such meaning is derived from the contrast of forms itself and from the range of possible situations in which each could be used. This might be characterised by describing the simple present form as 'dogmatic' usage and the present continuous as 'communicative'.

Lexical items are organised in sets which fall within certain conceptual limits. Each man's view of life is based on a conceptual field devised for himself or borrowed from others. His membership of a speech-community implies a recognition of a generalised pattern of concepts which he may share or reject. The relationship between the community's world-view and the structure of the lexical and formal items of their language is circular. It is impossible to say whether the body of concepts or the language is fundamentally dominant, they are so intertwined. Certainly in daily use the language structure dominates the structuring of this conceptual field because it formulates this field for its clearest contact with external phenomena. This has led certain anthropologists to maintain that the linguistic system of each language is itself the shaper of ideas. This is an extreme position. Many would give language a secondary rôle in this complex matter. The world-view comes first and the linguistic system is structured to represent it more or less well. For most members of the community the linguistic system leads, in turn, to some restructuring of the world-view. There is no alternative for most individual users of the language. The choice is between remaining silent and bending one's ideas to meet the categories of linguistic items available. The philosopher-poet may reorder and 'purify' his use of language—i.e. bring it into line with his analysis of the universe, but other members of the speech-community rarely. United action can occasionally make changes to (mainly) lexical items. This in part accounts for historical changes in language. It also explains the changes in emotional content of items at different times, such as the names of nationalities or races, such as grammatical features like 'I aint' and 'it is they'.

Within the extremes in any direction of the total conceptual field the linguistic items are strung. The lexical items formally defined as adjective and in the set referring to happiness in English are: content, blissful, blithe, cheerful, cheery, happy, merry, joyous, joyful, and possibly others. Their relationship one to the other is contrastive. 'Cheerful' 'means' what it does because it is contrasted with 'cheery', 'happy' and all the other items in the set. There are degrees of contrast. Clearly 'cheerful' contrasts graphically (and phonetically) less with 'cheery' than with the other items. The items also mean what they do because each can be used in a range of context and collocations which largely overlap (they belong to the same 'set', after all) but which also do *not* overlap. It is the extent to which they do not overlap which provides their 'meaning' within the set, and the extent to which the set does not overlap with all the other lexical sets of the language which provides the 'meaning' of the set. The relationships can be symbolised as follows:

The meaning of set A of lexical items is

$$(A+a)+(A+b)+(A+c)\ldots,$$

where A is the difference in contextual reference of all the items in the set from all the items of any other set of lexical items in the language; and a, b, c... is the difference between the contextual reference of each item and the reference of any other item in the set. There is further complexity in that an item may belong to several sets and its 'meaning' will also include contrast with the implications of membership of these other contrastive sets. A full analysis of the context references in the language would enable a lexicon of such items to be established. There is a similarity between the minimal contrasts symbolised here and the use of 'phoneme' and 'morpheme' in linguistic analysis. Detailed contextual analysis would make more useful the concept of '*sememe*' which some linguists have introduced.

The important thing for the language teacher to realise is that there can never be a precise 1 : 1 relationship between lexical items in two languages. The range covered by the items in a set may be similar in languages which have shared some cultural traditions, but the position of any one item within that set will be quite different. This is easily seen if it is borne in mind that the number of items in such a set will be different in one language from the number in a set in the other. In one $x$ items must do the work done by $y$ items in the other.

# 3. GENERAL LINGUISTICS AND APPLIED LINGUISTICS

The first two chapters will have given some idea of the range and complexity of language and its description. In many ways the study of language must be the foremost of the social sciences, for it deals with the expression of man's nature, and the tool he uses for his social organisation.

One of the greatest difficulties that has faced the study of language has been the need to work with and through language in the analysis of language itself. The procedures and the results of this analysis of language have had to be expressed in the language. For this reason modern linguistic analysis has made great use of symbols and mathematical procedures, thus avoiding for part of its work the need to prejudge its procedures by the structure imposed by language itself.

Like other social sciences, linguistics has needed to clarify its methods, stripping them of anecdotalism, and defining its terms of reference. This has been and will continue to be difficult, if not impossible, to the same extent as in other sciences, since intuition must play a large part in linguistic analysis. I know about language in general not primarily from observation of others but from my feelings about my own language. Further procedures of analysis will then be objectively controlled but it would be inefficient not to use (with care) the store of experience which each individual speaker (including the linguist) has within him on matters of language. If he is trained to observe, analyse and compare, then his intuition about his own language will be valuable.

Among the fields of linguistic study, the oldest is *philology*. Philology was concerned principally with an analysis of the development of each language and with the historical relationship of languages in language families. To this end certain 'laws' were propounded, notably the 'laws' of sound-change in the development of Germanic languages. Unlike scientific laws, of course, their application was not universal and they merely stated what had happened, being of no use as predictors. For the most part, however, the investigation of language was piecemeal and wholly subjective. There are still philological societies and students of philology, but the move towards formal, objective procedures in linguistic investigation has led away from that relaxed pursuit of a long-lost Indo-European language which characterised philology. Where the name persists it will probably be found to cover a rigorous pursuit of reality, as rigorous as any linguistic scientist could demand.

*Historical* (or *diachronic*) *linguistics* deals with the successive stages of development of languages. It is closely associated with *comparative linguistics*, which is concerned with the comparison from one or a number of points of view of two or more languages. Contrastive studies may form part of this work, providing information about the areas of possible interference by the native language of the foreign language learner. These two branches of general linguistics share many of the techniques of modern *descriptive linguistics*. The latter discipline, aspects of which have been the main concern of the previous chapter, may be characterised by its application of scientific rigour to the analysis of language. While recognising the place of intuition, descriptive linguists demand that every statement made about linguistic features be subject to cross-checking and continuing modification in the direction of increasing delicacy and economy.

It is in this respect that general linguistics today differs from the philology of old. Whereas the linguistic scientist will consider his task completed when he has presented the analysis and resulting description, the true philologist would consider it his duty to include judgments of language based on historical or philosophical principles. The descriptive linguist may offer his views on the efficiency or elegance of what he describes, but not within the terms of his description.

Descriptive linguistics is concerned essentially with contemporary language. Clearly, descriptions thus formulated will be of use to historical linguistics as language changes. Descriptive linguistics normally makes *synchronic* statements about language at one given time as a self-contained system of communication. Historical linguistics makes *diachronic* linguistic statements comparing features of the same language at different points in time.

It will be apparent from the ground covered in the previous chapter that general linguistics, and particularly descriptive linguistics, uses the findings of one or two disciplines which have a separate existence. *Acoustic phonetics* and *physiology* contribute to the study of the production and perception of the sounds of language, as well as providing information about the possible range of such sound in human language. The overlap between these studies and linguistics is considerable. The purely linguistic areas can only be defined when all the sounds within any one language have been described.

*Semantics* is the study of meaning, and since meaning is a characteristic of all sign and symbol systems it obviously has a far wider application than to language. Certain current philosophical semantic theories have received no attention in this book since, in their turn, they belong outside a linguistic study which aims at scientific rigour. Most linguists at present prefer a formal or contextual description of meaning and these are certainly of more value to the language teacher. Intuitively felt meaning may be used as a cross-reference at some stage in an investigation but the description itself will work with observable form. 'Form underlies meaning.'

A number of related disciplines are grouped under the name of *applied linguistics*. The term was originally used to refer to general linguistics in its application to language teaching. It is still used in this restricted sense in the United States, although the increasingly obvious relationship between a number of fields where the findings and data of general linguistics have an application is leading to an extension of the reference of the term.

Within language teaching itself, a number of related disciplines are clearly of great interest. We want to know the interconnexion of language and thought in the minds of speakers of the *target language*, the language being learnt, just as we must know about our students in their relation to their own and the target language. For this information we look to *psycholinguistics*. Very often psycholinguistics has, like psychology and psychiatry, been concerned with what is abnormal rather than what is normal in human language and behaviour. There is much to be done in the study of bilingualism and in those questions of national and racial prejudice which are conditioned by and expressed through language.

Any attempt to describe meaning partly in terms of its contextualisation, as well as any claim to lead the student into a second 'culture' through language, must depend on an analysis of the foreign society and the social implications of its language. The relationship of language to primitive study has received a great deal of attention in *ethnolinguistic* and anthropological linguistic studies. Comparatively little has been done on language in advanced societies. *Sociolinguistics* is coming to replace the other terms as more attention is given to the relationship of all language to the respective societies and to the establishment of general principles of investigation. One urgent problem that faces applied linguists is the language problem in developing nations. Efficiency and economic considerations as well as national unity may make the raising to a dominant position of one of a number of competing languages a necessity. It is in this field that the linguist will need to offer prescriptive advice since he must decide for one variety of the language, for one source language, for the creation of neologisms, for the administrative and other prescriptive means of establishing the chosen language. For this prescriptive aspect of applied linguistics the term *institutional linguistics* is sometimes used.

Descriptive linguistics may be applied as an aid to literary analysis. It is, of course, no substitute for the aesthetic judgment of literature, but linguistics can bring the kind of aid which historical studies offer the critic; it can set the work within its linguistic background, both diachronic and synchronic. *Stylistic*, or more properly, *linguostylistic* analysis can show the linguistic mechanism used by the author and the extent to which he diverged in practice from the linguistic norms of his time.

*Automatic translation* (or 'M.T.' for *machine translation*) is concerned with linguistics in its application to the fields of cybernetics and information storage and retrieval. Work on automatic translation dates only from 1946 and work on information processing is no older; the design of mechanical computers is rather older. The development of electronic computers, with immensely larger storage and with enormously greater speeds, has increased the possibilities in this field. It is certain that the discoveries of workers in machine translation will be as important for linguistics as the latter will be for M.T.

# 4. LANGUAGE LEARNING

We are all students of psychology, for we think and react, and we probably think about our behaviour occasionally.

Psychology has hitherto played little part in the study of language and its use. Most attention has been given to verbal learning, but usually with nonsense syllables, rarely with systematic language items. Moreover, psychologists have been most interested in the abnormalities of human thinking and behaviour. If, however, we want to make language learning more efficient and to bring foreign learners nearer to native proficiency we need to be aware of the psychological investigation of normal learning and of normal linguistic behaviour.

Psychology in its early days was plagued, as were all 'social sciences', by a surfeit of 'anecdotalism'. An individual's awareness of his own thought and physical processes, expressed in descriptive terms, would regularly serve as the basis for deductions about the behaviour of people in general. In its attempts to reach the status of a science, psychology has tended to go to the other extreme, completely rejecting 'insight'. Nevertheless, 'insight' has always played, and will continue to play, a very important part in all the 'social sciences'.

The most influential of the early work carried out was that of Thorndike and Pavlov. Both were concerned with the relationship between a stimulus and the resultant action in the organism under study. Experiments were concerned with establishing the conditions for increasing the probability of a recurrence of a given response or with extending the stimulation preceding the occurrence of the given response by associating a number of conditioned stimuli with the original stimulus. Reward (or the avoidance of pain) was found to be an important element in establishing the various stimulus-response relationships or in preventing their disappearance.

Behavioural psychology imposed a discipline on investigation by concerning itself only with the existence of stimulus and response and with the observable conditions for their association. There are close similarities, of course, between the behaviour which Thorndike and Pavlov were endeavouring to induce and the behaviour which the language teacher is likely to hope for, at least in the elementary stages of language learning. In no subject is the dialogue of stimulus and response so much part of the behaviour aimed at.

B. F. Skinner belongs clearly to the behaviourist school. He has taken an extreme view, rejecting insight altogether, and concerning himself solely with what is observable. Much more important, he has established principles which have been the basis for the design of most of the simple teaching machines and which lie at the root of most language-teaching material now being produced. He has emphasised the close relationship of response and reinforcement. The latter comes to be associated with the particular response, or group of responses, to a given stimulus or group of stimuli. In Skinner's theory the process is as follows: an object is present or an event occurs; the organism emits a response (for reason or merely by chance); the response affects the environment; the environment rewards the organism—with food (primary reinforcement) or with praise, money (secondary reinforcement).

Thorndike, Pavlov and Skinner have shown the possibility of extending the number of stimuli and the number of responses related by association. A further important possibility demonstrated in the work of each of them is that of training the organism in finer and finer discrimination by the contrast of increasingly similar items and by withholding and presenting of rewards on an increasingly specific basis.

The behaviourists have been concerned with the relationship of *items*, whether single words or single pulls on a rope. Language teaching, of course, is concerned primarily with integrated skills. Nevertheless, the work of the behaviourists has relevance to the language teacher's job.

From Skinner's theory of *operant conditioning* we learn that an 'increase of operant strength' (a term considered more appropriate, because less emotive, than 'learning') depends on:

the breaking up of the information or behaviour to be taught at each step into the smallest possible size;
the involvement of the learner and the requirement of some positive action from him;
the immediate confirmation of the learner's success.

The clearest application of these principles is to be seen in the criteria for the construction of linear teaching programmes and in the design of language teaching drills. I shall return to a consideration of Skinner's theory of 'operant conditioning' at a later point in this chapter, when I come to consider linear teaching programmes.

The title of neobehaviourists has occasionally been given to more recently established work on the stimulus-response-reinforcement relationship. This work has endeavoured to discover the processes in between the three stages in this relationship. It has underlined the rôle of groups of reactions and their association with complexes of environmental stimuli. Although there is the same fundamental stimulus-response-reinforcement in this set of theories, there is also a recognition of the complexity of reactions and of secondary stimuli which in turn arouse merely a part of the total (potential) response to the event or object which provided the primary stimulus. Whatever the intermediate processes which such neobehaviourist work may be trying to discover between stimulus and response, it is the extremes of this learning situation which are of interest to the teacher. What is important is that work on these intermediate variables has led to a view of secondary stimuli and reinforcement which is explicitly closer to the theories of *gestalt psychology* than are those of the earlier behaviourists. The neobehaviourist pays more attention to the part played by complexity and the interrelationships of the more obviously related stimulus and response chains. The gestalt psychologist differs from this only in the priority he gives to the effect of the total functioning of the behaviour under investigation.

The behaviourists and neobehaviourists have always held that the selection of the correct response by the learner is initially random, trial and error, although clearly the randomness of selection will be limited by the relationship of the S-R item to previous items and the resultant bias in favour of the selection of the best response. Nevertheless, the limitation on randomness is a result of the (external) chain of items (=programme). The situation within the organism (no concern of the psychologist as far as Skinner is concerned) is largely unbiased towards any of the possible responses except as a result of the preceding items.

The gestalt psychologists, on the other hand, have recognised the importance of the learner's 'insight', helped by intelligence and experience. They have emphasised the importance of the recognition by the learner of a complex goal to which he has a 'set' (favourable attitudes) or not. Success at each stage confirms the expectancy of goal-achievement.

In gestalt theories the total environment is central to the learning process; it is more than the sum of the S-R items into which it can be analysed. Part of this 'behavioural environment' is the learner's recognition of a complex goal and his progress towards its achievement. It is not enough, as the Skinnerians believe, to break up the teaching matter into its smallest constituent parts. Such an analysis, for the gestalt psychologist, ignores the significance which the whole act gives to its parts.

Clearly these concepts are more in tune with the needs of the language learner. During much of his learning the S-R procedure may be sufficient. Frequently though and especially as he nears the end of his course, he needs a complex of skills. He needs to be ready, precisely, to move in a (foreign) behavioural environment. Moreover, the learner in language learning more than most others needs to see and understand his goal. The adult learner will work to a highly complex and well-described goal; the child will need a somewhat less complex goal. Even in the earliest years at school, however, the child is no longer operating in the S-R process which for the youngest babies is sufficient. By the time he reaches school age the child is influenced more by his total (class) environment and needs to have some awareness of short-term achievement possibilities.

One very new development from gestalt psychology is the neo-field theory of behaviour. It suggests that total physical response leads to more efficient learning than does partial physical response. Investigations are promising inasmuch as they have been concerned principally with foreign language learning, but not enough work has been carried out for any firm conclusions to be drawn. It seems likely, however, that it may give scientific support to noisy, busy language rooms, and this will be no bad thing.

Neuropsychological investigations are unlikely to be of great importance for language teaching. In many ways the language teacher has a position similar to that of the purest behaviourists. He or she will not be uninterested in, but will have little use for, the processes which intervene between presentation of stimulus material and production of the correct response by the learner unless knowledge of these intermediate processes will enable him to improve the learning conditions and to increase his students' motivation.

In two previous chapters I have mentioned new approaches to language classification and language description which are essentially operational. In the case of transformational generative grammar no pretence is made that this is *the* way that native speakers generate and recognise well-formed sentences; it simply aims at setting up a descriptive system comparable to native intuition because it works entirely with acceptable sentences and leads inevitably, within its own terms, to the production of equally well-formed sentences. In the description of constituents of a notional language, attention is being given to a functional classification (register) as well as to a geographical classification (dialect).

It may well be that a similar operational approach to the psychology of learning may be more productive than a precise attention to the actual internal phenomena of learning. It is possible that a model drawn from information processing may be valuable. It would have the advantage of regarding the human learning process in objective, mechanistic terms. At the same time it would provide a global motivation in terms of the successful processing of incoming information. An operational description in terms of information processing or cybernetics would allow the methodologist of language learning to concentrate on the establishment of the best conditions for bridging the gap between the beginning and the achievement of whatever proficiency is required.

The danger of any theories treating human learning at the level of item is that they make no allowance for personality or for the application of intelligence. Much of the work on language teaching material is in terms of item. Indeed part of this book will be dealing with teaching at this level of material. Not only does small-step, item progression provide material for special language learning at many stages of the course, but its construction imposes a valuable discipline on the teacher's attitude to the material and to the student.

Nevertheless, there must be frequent calls on the deductive powers of the learner, and I shall be outlining suggestions for such work in chapters 5 and 7.

The student may not like foreigners in general or the speakers of the target language in particular. He may have speech inhibitions. These and other factors are usually overlooked in accounting for failure, just as their opposites are left out of account in assessing the reasons for success in language learning. These and a host of other factors deriving from the student's personal history establish in him a 'set' to language learning, attitudes which are modified by factors within the course.

Motivation is a combination of all these in dynamic relationship with his work. The complexity of this factor is in itself an explanation of the small amount of attention usually paid to it. Measurement of attitude might usefully form part of aptitude tests. Although little could be done to adjust conditions to the findings of such tests it would be of advantage to know all the reasons for success or failure.

Without going into the nature of the course or the range of language teaching material, it is possible to consider the personal factors, apart from motivation, which will influence the efficiency of the learning. Let us assume that the aim is full, all-round proficiency in the foreign language.

Visual and aural perception are physical aptitudes with no large intellectual component. Yet they are highly important to language learning. Indeed one study of underachievement in language learning has emphasised the critical importance of auditory and visual ability. Closely combined with visual and aural perception are visual and aural comprehension. This is the ability to sequence single sounds, or single utterances, single images into a meaningful whole and to extend the content (or 'to read between the lines').

Child learners differ from adult learners in many ways. Their attention is of a shorter duration, they are quite differently motivated and their interests are less specialised. In terms of physical ability it is probably in the area of visual and aural comprehension that there are the greatest differences between child and adult learner. It is in every teacher's and parent's experience that children go through stages of listing items in one picture, classifying the events in each picture before they come to see the connexion between pictures and then to preface or extend the total content of the sequence of pictures.

Reading and writing speeds, in the native language and at a level of content well within the student's ability, are physical abilities with a large intellectual component. Fluency and accuracy of speech (in terms of his normal performance in his own native speech) have a negative rather than positive contribution to language learning; they can inhibit control of a language and may prevent the achievement of full proficiency.

Memory is of two types: 'rote' memory and 'immediate' memory (which may, in turn, be a combination of a number of factors mentioned already). Inevitably, language learning must depend on some ability to store items, whether by straightforward learning by heart or by association with other items and other abilities.

There is a higher intellectual component in the ability to reason, the ability to deal in words (often called 'verbal intelligence') and structures, very similar to the previous ability. These abilities are certainly not a *sine qua non* of language learning, although they may well increase considerably the efficiency of learning and enable short cuts to be taken. On the other hand, it is possible for learning to take place with reasonable efficiency when these abilities are not highly developed, and course material should be developed to meet all needs. Variety of ability of this kind presents difficulties in the normal class situation and here is the case for material designed to allow for a variety of aptitudes and abilities and for the development of equipment to make the presentation of such a variety possible.

It is fundamental to the new approach to language learning that any normal human being can learn a human language, and that any failure to do so reflects far more on the teaching material and the physical conditions than on the learner. The degree of proficiency that the learner attains, and the rate at which he learns, will vary according to his abilities and aptitudes, but this variation will show far more in relation to the learner's approach to a near-native proficiency and less at a level which may be loosely described as that of 'communication'.

A high efficiency of learning will depend on matching material and means to individual needs. The ability to do this will in turn depend on the establishment of the learner's 'profile' by measuring his aptitudes and abilities. The prognostic and aptitude test will undoubtedly become a regular feature of language teaching, but these tests will be the subject of another chapter.

The terms *programme* and *programming* are very widely used. These words are fine examples of *polysemy* by way of varied contextual situations. Almost certainly the first meaning of 'programme' was through association with certain psychological theories of learning, most clearly that of Skinner. Professor Carroll has characterised teaching programmes as needing to possess all four of the following attributes:

1. Programmed instruction must be based on an adequate specification of the 'terminal behaviour' aimed at;
2. the material of instruction must be organized and presented in a carefully designed sequence of steps so that each step is, to the greatest extent possible, made easier by virtue of the material learned in previous steps;
3. steps must be of the right size for the student to master readily;
4. the student must have the opportunity of testing his control of each critical step as he proceeds through the programme, responses being confirmed immediately or the student being led to understand and to correct his error.

Items 3 and 4 in this specification are the ones most open to dispute amongst protagonists of programmed learning, 4 because it places the onus of testing and error-correction on the student rather than on the material, and 3 because it is so vague.

The terms 'programme' and 'programming' have also been associated with the hardware developed by workers in programmed learning, the teaching machines. These machines provide control over the student's progress through the material. However, they have been quite expensive and have certainly inhibited the use of these methods. Recent investigations, however, have shown that the *scrambled book*, which can perform the functions of the teaching machine, is as effective as the teaching machine. Moreover, it has been shown that 'cheating' (looking at the correct response before making it), the possibility of which has been taken as one of the main disadvantages of the book as against the machine, is certainly not harmful, and may even contribute to learning.

The 'programme' most often refers to the material, constructed more or less on the principles of careful programming and available in scrambled book form or for use on certain types of teaching machine. Anyone faced with a so-called 'programmed course' would do well to apply the first two principles stated above, questioning particularly the nature of the responses called for, and their relationship to the total terminal behaviour (which is presumably stated in explicit terms in the accompanying literature).

Traditional class teaching has aimed at the same techniques as programmed learning, but, for a number of reasons, with very varying success. The teacher has first of all an overall plan of his lesson, presumably in its turn part of the overall aim of his course ('terminal behaviour'), although probably not defined. At the beginning of his teaching session he makes a statement, presents a picture or takes other action to stimulate his student to respond in a certain way (principle 2, above). The student makes a response. If the response is what the teacher wanted, the student receives confirmation (a smile, the absence of reproach). The student consigns the response to his memory store. If the response is not as expected, on the other hand, the teacher will alter his overall plan to take account of this (principle 4).

In practice, the class situation is rarely like this because there are many students. Response cannot be taken from every student every time. In any case the teacher would find it impossible to 'process' many responses and to make a tactical decision based on all of them. Nor can confirmation be given to all the students.

The answer suggested by programmed learning is for each student to have access to material which has been carefully designed. Such material will be so arranged that the probability of each student making the correct response is very high indeed (*linear programme*), or several alternative programmes will be available and the student will be referred to these in accordance with the errors he makes (*branching programme*).

Each unit (*frame*) of the linear programme contains a stimulus (statement or picture, etc.) and calls for the student to complete a response statement (*constructed response*).

|  | range  Les lettres qu'il avait  rangées sur le banc<br>trouve  Les lettres qu'il avait                     sur le banc |
|---|---|
| trouvées |  |

Fig. 8. A constructed response frame typical of a linear programme.

In the linear programme, progress is in one direction, and steps from frame to frame are consistent in size. Moreover, *one* unit of information only is taught before the student is asked to complete a response. The scheme of the linear programme is

$$A \rightarrow B \rightarrow C \rightarrow D \rightarrow E \rightarrow$$

where A–E show frames of the type illustrated in figure 8.

The branching (or *intrinsic*) programme, developed essentially by Crowder, makes greater use of student differences. Whereas the Skinner programme presents the material in the smallest possible quantity, steps so small that individual student differences become unimportant, the Crowder programme uses student error as part of the teaching process. Each frame in the branching programme

---

Frame 15

Il avait *rangé* les lettres sur le banc
Les lettres qu'il avait rangées sur le banc

There is a change in the spelling of *rangé*.
You will notice that the letters 'es' have been
added when 'rangées' comes after 'les lettres'
instead of in front. Of course you know that
the singular of 'les lettres' is '*la* lettre'.

| Les pantoufles qu'il avait | frame 20<br>mis | sous la table |
|---|---|---|
|  | frame 16<br>mises |  |
|  | frame 14<br>miss |  |

---

Fig. 9. A frame from a branching programme.

consists of more than the minimum of information and the student is then asked to choose from one of a number of possible responses (*multiple choice*).

Figure 9 shows a very unsatisfactory teaching method. Indeed, readers will by now realise that this example runs counter to the principles which this book is trying to illustrate. It serves, however, to show the inapplicability of the Crowder programme to the teaching of formal items in the foreign language. It can be used to teach *about* language only. Language proficiency and language teaching have little use for the disquisitions which are applicable in other subjects. Nevertheless, the small step of the Skinner programme may be combined with the design principles and the multiple choice technique of the Crowder programme. Such combination of these two approaches has been an important part of the work of Pressey.

The scheme of a typical branching programme might be as follows:

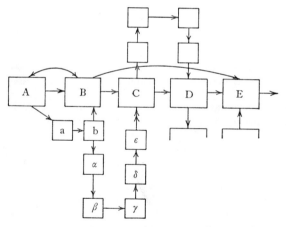

Fig. 10. A branching programme.

The central programme is A–E. At frame A a student may be referred to frame B, or may be taken through a short remedial branch (a, b) (*wash ahead*). At b in this sub-programme the student may be led back to frame B or may be taken on to a longer remedial branch which will bring him to C. The student at frame B may be referred (*wash back*) to the initial frame or may bypass frames C and D. The path to be followed at each frame will be determined by the multiple choice response selected.

Bypassing of frames, of course (*skip-frame* or *forward branching* programme), is a feature which can be incorporated in the linear programme given that multiple choice response provides a selection device.

---

Frame 15

    Il avait *rangé* les lettres sur le banc

    Les lettres qu'il avait *rangé*es sur le banc
    Les lettres qu'il avait *trouvé*es sur le banc
    Les lettres qu'il avait *mis*es sur le banc

| Les lettres qu'il avait | frame 16 | sur le banc |
| | étalées | |
| | frame 3 | |
| | étallées | |
| | frame 14 | |
| | étalé | |

---

Fig. 11. A frame from a modified branching programme.

There is no doubt that the written teaching programme can be of value in the teaching of the graphological features of a language. As such, however, they can only be partial since the major part of the language learning will be oral. Moreover, the relation between pronunciation and spelling is often close enough for the phonology of the language to be of help in teaching the graphology.

By their stress on the importance of knowing (in linguistic terms) the aim and content of the teaching, and by their insistence on ensuring that each unit of information is of digestible size and self-confirming, the new oral techniques of language teaching have more in common with 'programming' than many realise.

As in many other aspects of language learning, the position is not one of Skinner *or* Crowder, but that of using either, or a combination of both, as appropriate. The 'operant conditioning' view of learning regards the student response as part of the learning process; the branching programme uses the response merely as an indicator of the student's needs. Both will be used in future language course design.

The incorporation of visual presentation devices offers one possible development of immense interest to language teaching. The *spectrograph* has long been used in departments of phonetics for research and teaching in pronunciation. The visual demonstration of sound can help in pronunciation since the student is shown how far he is deviating from the performance aimed at, particularly when the target performance is shown at the same time.

Work in the United States has been directed to the development of a teaching machine on these lines. Both at Harvard and the University of Michigan such machines have been used in teaching pronunciation. At Michigan the work of the Speech Auto-Instructional Device (SAID) is being extended to deal with segmental features.

In Britain one of the language laboratories at Cambridge University is equipped with closed-circuit television, and this will serve both teaching and research directed towards the development of audio-visual teaching devices and the design of material using to the full the contribution of visual presentation.

Even further in the future lies the full development of *adaptive* programmes. The branched programme anticipates as reliably as it can the nature of each learner's difficulty and the type of error he will produce. Skinnerians would object, of course, that this anticipation leads to the building in of error and sets up conflict between the aims of careful course design and the provision of accurate remedial material.

On the other hand, the supporters of adaptive programming would maintain that the design of good teaching material *must* anticipate a significant rate of error on the part of the learner. Indeed the adaptive programme will adapt on the basis of the rise or fall of the learner's rate of error.

The teacher's traditional abhorrence of error *of any kind* has weakened the efficiency of a lot of teaching. Its rejection has left unconsidered the various types of error. The learner's errors are not all of the same kind. In language they will range from calques of the native language which are utterly foreign to the language being learnt, to errors which might well be made by the educated native speakers of the foreign language through carelessness or the momentary aberration which, cumulatively, leads eventually to linguistic change, which is respectable enough!

Not only has error not been used as a source of information and an indication of the lines of a change of teaching programme but its motivating power has been overlooked. Any view which regards goal-achievement as important to learning will consider most types of error as being as highly motivating as success, and, therefore, as making a positive contribution to learning.

Discrimination training has hitherto not played an extensive part in even the most advanced language material. Teaching on the basis of contrasts is essentially discrimination training, but the term is normally reserved for work at a very delicate level. If I teach by contrasting 'he wants some books (he likes reading)' and 'he wants any books (he reads everything)' or 'it's gold (put it in the safe)' and 'it's cold (put it by the fire)' I am teaching discrimination, but only at the level, respectively, of lexical item and phoneme.

The work of the behaviourists suggests that training at greater degrees of delicacy is possible by taking the learner through a series of increasingly fine distinctions and by employing the normal means of reinforcement. In this way it is possible to reach a high level of allophonic, intonational and grammatical discrimination. Indeed, Rand Morton has produced such a course as an introduction to Spanish. It is possible to reach a near-native standard of pronunciation by taking the learner through pairs of contiguous sounds in the native and foreign languages and then phonemic and allophonic distinctions in the foreign language. On a solid basis of this kind of ear training it is possible to build a high degree of efficiency.

Time is always limited, however, and priorities have to be established. Inevitably, the greatest attention is given to the phonemic, lexical and grammatical aspects of the foreign language, since it is in these areas that a breakdown of communication is possible. The discrimination of *k*ing and *c*all though desirable is not essential, since the distinction is never phonemic.


# 5. LANGUAGE TEACHING

The objectives of language teaching are many and varied. The foreign language may be part of a course which considers only the cultural, educational aspect (defined in many ways) of the language component. Courses of this kind are probably still the most common throughout the world and at every level of the educational system. They may be subject to examination or may be subject to a pattern of content which has to be shared with other academic but non-linguistic studies.

In the primary school the objective will be to use the language and to use it for its own sake, since the learners will have no firm opinions on the matter as long as the circumstances are pleasant and involve activity. The purpose behind the teaching may be functional, in a bilingual situation or near a frontier, or where adaptation to a foreign environment is urgent (for example, as a result of immigration); the purpose may be psychological: the use of the best age for language learning.

In the non-examination classes of the secondary school, too, the purposes may be similar, but the foreign language is more likely to be taught in the same way as in the examination classes because both types of class will have the same teacher, or teachers with the same training, be bound by the same regulations, or because the school tradition must be observed in all the school classes. It is likely, moreover, that these classes will in time be required to sit an examination designed for them, and the new examination, however enlightened, will decide the content of the course. It is to be hoped that such new examinations will avoid the pitfalls which beset the established language examinations and to which I shall refer in the next chapter.

In adult education the possibilities are wider. Not only are there examination classes; there are also the recreational language classes, a medley of the practical and the cultural.

A growing amount of language teaching is directed at groups who have a clear purpose in mind. Whether adolescents with a fairly precise idea of the job they want, or businessmen and administrators with specific jobs to do, or even the traveller and holidaymaker, the emphasis is on language as a tool. More and more of the tourist's classes are treating language in this way and are taking over from the recreational classes which have served the potential tourist in the past.

Time is at the heart of the problems language teaching has to face. Ideally one could wish for a student's lifetime! The teacher and course designer must use all the motivation and relevance possible and must ensure that the teaching material contains no superfluous linguistic items.

Selection of linguistic content, situations, and subjects of presentation is essential. The adult specialist must be equipped to perform a limited number of tasks within a particular rôle. How near an approach can be made to this aim will depend on the homogeneity of interests within a class. This emphasis on specialist functions is an important requirement. It does not deny the full aim of any language course: to bring speaking, understanding, reading and writing to a level in keeping with performance in the learner's native language. In particular skills, especially reading speed, the native language performance may indeed be surpassed.

These two sets of aims are not contradictory. Every language teacher must *aim* at the second set in all his teaching. He needs to compromise by restricting the number of language skills, and by limiting the lexical and grammatical items in the course on the basis of comparative usefulness. With limited time available, restrictions of this kind allow a higher standard of proficiency to be maintained than if the range of work were not thus limited. Partial work of this kind must nevertheless be part (or capable of being part) of a complete, high-level proficiency course. The relationship should be so clear that supplementary work of a similarly high level would be possible.

The danger in language teaching has always been to regard a time-limited course as in some way complete. This leads to the attempt to cram every possible linguistic item in the inventory of the language into the time available, with a concern rather for the number of such items than for a high proficiency with a carefully selected, integrated number of items. A course crammed like a badly packed suitcase not only deals unsatisfactorily with a large number of items: its other characteristic is the inability to add any further work, should extra class sessions present themselves, or to reduce content rationally should this become necessary.

It is important to define the adult learner's needs on the basis of a full job-description. Where all four skills are required, the relative importance of any of them may vary. There may even be a specialist requirement for another skill, say that of interpreting or translating. The scientist may need a high proficiency in reading comprehension and perhaps some proficiency in aural comprehension of certain styles or the scientific register of the language. The salesman will need primarily a speaking proficiency and perhaps writing proficiency within the styles of persuasion and instruction in the target language. Within this range he will need considerably more attention to his pronunciation than is customary, if he is to win friends and sell more.

Young children will need speaking and understanding proficiency within the registers of play; the older child will want primarily aural comprehension and reading comprehension since he is more intent on discovering things; the young adolescent, unless he is preparing for a specialisation, will want speaking, understanding and reading. He will only need a high proficiency in writing if future studies will clearly require it.

Language teaching is essentially the handing over of skills. It has long been regarded as the passing on of information and this is still often the attitude of language teachers. Many teachers would disagree with remarks written by Politzer and Staubach: 'rules are the description of the student's own performance. *Rules ought to be summaries of behaviour*. They function only secondarily as "predictors".'

There is, of course, a certain satisfaction in treating a subject of study as though it consists only of a corpus of knowledge which can be parcelled, graded and handed over, so many discrete items at a time, until the weekly test or terminal examination provides a tidy measure, where a lexical item earns as good a mark as the correct use of a verbal form. Language involves complexes of sub-skills and it is in this complexity that language learning differs from other skills, such as car driving, dancing or swimming. Whereas most skills involve but a part of the human being, the use of language calls for the contribution of the whole personality.

In most teaching situations teachers and students face one another. It is clearly a development of the tutorial situation, with authoritarian overtones of 'us' and 'them'. It is a situation in which a dialogue *might* take place but no such dialogue takes place; there is rarely much feedback at all, because there are too many potential sources of feedback to be of much help. Efficiency of teaching demands that communication be one-way.

This face-to-face situation is possible where material is merely being presented, but in language such presentation should usually be short-lived, as I shall endeavour to show.

Sitting a class in a full circle and taking one's place at the circumference, or at the centre, overcomes the gap between teacher and taught. This arrangement also helps to create the group-feeling which is an important dynamic in language teaching. Its principal disadvantage is that it does not easily allow the teacher to resume his focal position; the arrangement functions in one mode, that in which the teacher can be less apparent than the 'community' he has created.

I want for the moment to leave the subject of classroom arrangement and to consider the types of activity which may be required in the language classroom. The stages of a session might well be as follows:

*Presentation* of a dialogue or other situational text. The close relationship of meaning and context of situation has been considered in an earlier chapter. As an introduction to the unit of material the presentation text serves to interest the students and to provide a situation on and around which the forms to be learnt can be built and practised. At this stage it is the material that is carrying the main burden. However constructed and however presented, its clarity, relevance and motivating power are a matter of earlier preparation. For this reason the bipolar arrangement of class and teacher (or tape) is suitable since the only feedback necessary from the class will be to ensure that full attention is on the material being presented and that boredom is not setting in.

*Stabilisation.* The presentation text has been displayed to the class, perhaps two or three times, as a global whole, and the passive stage will have been very short. Now comes the need to engage learners in the situation, by repeating utterances, by contradicting or answering the teacher's statements with appropriate utterances, by acting out the whole or parts of it, adapting it to re-create more or less parallel situations, until all the students control the original material fully.

At this stage it will be necessary to change the pattern of relationships from teacher (or tape) to class, with irregular feedback, to class to teacher (until the teacher becomes of little significance). Reinforcement is, of course, a continuing process at this second stage, as at others, but it is necessary to revert from time to time to the bipolar arrangement so that drilling (an authoritarian practice) may take place. Already it can be seen that there is a need for flexibility in the class arrangement.

In the next stages, *fluency practice* or *conversation*, where the material is completely transferred to the students, who use it to express their personalities or their assumed personalities, the class will need to act as a group and to work in smaller sub-groups.

Parallel to these activities, drilling of grammatical and phonological patterns will take place. This work is best suited to the language laboratory but no such equipment may be available, and, in any case, some classroom preparation may be required. The classroom arrangements must allow the bipolar duologue situation to alternate with the withdrawal of the teacher's presence as in the second stage described above. An echelon or semi-circular class arrangement offers the most flexible system.

I have been considering the broad outline of the lesson plan and classroom situations which would be suitable for audio-lingual or audio-visual teaching. If we carry out a description of most learners' needs and an analysis of work requirements we shall undoubtedly find that the greatest demand is for speaking and listening proficiency.

The work analysis will normally show that writing proficiency is required only in relationship to the spoken language. Very seldom is any stylistic ability required. Most writing needs will be in terms of messages and reports in an informal register. In addition, some proficiency in the highly specialised activity of commercial correspondence may be necessary.

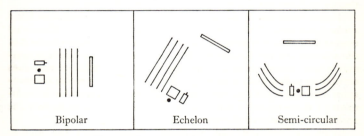

Fig. 12. Language class arrangement.

Language has its roots in its spoken forms. Its essentially dynamic nature is founded on the interplay of its spoken forms in all its social and communicating functions. The written language is only one of the multiple faces of language. Its extension through calligraphy and typography and through the stylistic variations in prose and verse, but above all its permanence, may well make of it the most admired of all the forms of a language.

Until the advent of recording equipment it was impossible to give the same permanence to the spoken language, and extremely difficult to convey the nature of individual greatness in the use of the spoken language, since any such memorialisation needed to be expressed in the written language. Language teaching has been influenced by all this and by its traditionally close association with the classics, the spoken analogues of which can never be more than partially revealed.

The priorities between spoken and written forms are clear when language is intended as a tool for a particular job. The nature of modern language itself imposes a priority even where the course is aiming at proficiency in all four major language skills. To teach first the written language is to teach little more than one register of the language, though it is a register in which great things are possible in the hands of gifted individuals with a highly developed language proficiency.

To teach first the spoken language ensures that the foundations of skill and knowledge are set in the dynamic area of language. Inevitably the spoken language is the more difficult, since work must be at a number of linguistic levels at once. Stress, intonation, phonemic and allophonic phonology have a counterpart in the written language in the graphemics alone: the formation of word shapes and attendant punctuation and other devices.

Writing systems in all languages which have them depict the spoken language. The relationship is normally one-way. The social uses of language rely heavily on the spoken language, as do most of the communicating functions. The written language offers permanence and is used to record the consensus, the result of activities carried on in the spoken language. Very rare is the reverse relationship. Moreover, the extension of telephones, radio and the development of voice-impelled teleprinters will emphasise still further the spoken language over the written language.

Language teaching will normally proceed from the spoken language to the written language. The material is presented by tape-recorder or in a language laboratory. Any normal human being can deal with the sounds of human language. The degree of delicacy in discrimination and pronunciation varies with the anticipated physical difficulties, resulting principally from the unwillingness of vocal organs of which the native language habits have made no use, but also from the absence of practice in distinguishing sounds unused in the native language.

A large amount of this work will overcome the adult learner's objections that he 'cannot hear' or 'does not know how it's spelt'. What the learner means is that all his previous education has conditioned him to trust his eyes rather than his ears. It will be found that intensive practice will prove to the objector that he is wrong. If he is the one in a hundred who really cannot discriminate, then he needs medical attention and must temporarily deny himself the pleasure of learning any but the written language.

The teacher must show his positive convictions, otherwise his doubts will show! For some years yet he may well be teaching language against the mainstream of other education if he believes that the first acquaintance with language must be in terms of sound. With younger children there will be no difficulty. With older children and adults the teacher must know his methods and trust them, refusing to relent, refusing to be drawn into an early introduction of

written forms or any *explanations* of utterances, until the learners
see for themselves that they can deal with spoken language.

The introduction of written forms at too early a date will invali-
date the approach through the spoken language and, backed by the
nature of the rest of education, will revive the suggestion that
spoken language is an impoverished relation of the written language.
The offer of explanations will also change the 'set' of the students
so that they begin to think that they should be hearing and talking
*about* the language. These are dangers which the teacher must avoid
if he is not to revert to the traditional situation, away from language
use.

The introduction of the written language need be delayed only
until it is clear that the learners regard the material before them as
primarily contextualised and formalised sound. After that the
moment to start connecting what is known to written marks on
paper will depend on the foreign language and the regularity (not
the accuracy) with which it marks down its spoken forms.

Meaning arises from formal contrasts within the language and
contextual contrasts with reality. 'Vous voulez bien du thé?' contrasts formally with 'Voulez-vous du thé?' (as do the English
sentences 'Do you want some tea?' with 'Do you want any tea?')
but the difference in meaning depends on a contrast between the
range of contexts in which each would be acceptable. Similarly, the
formal contrast of 'Do you want some sandwiches?' and 'Do you
want any sandwiches?' is less important to understanding than
contrast within the range of situations in which each would be
appropriate. The teacher and the course designer must use both the
formal contrasts and the contrast of characteristic, representative
contexts.

Context can be presented in one of three ways, by explanation,
by translation, or by illustration. The utterances of the presentation
text must interplay in such a way that they highlight certain developments within the total situation. Moreover, there will be transfer
from previous texts, since no lesson other than the first exists in
isolation. Nevertheless, the main burden of immediate situational
understanding will rest on explanation, translation or illustration.

Translation will suggest that the foreign situation exists only in
terms of the native language. Potentially, in fact it opens the way
to all the emotive associations of the native language and, with older
children and adults, promises a return to the grammar-translation
methods of earlier instruction. Explanation in the native language
is only less harmful in so far as it is clearly a summary and as

such will not suggest that the foreign language situation can only be acting as a substitute for the full native language text.

The most common illustration in the language classroom is the all-in-one wall picture, in which everything is happening at once in the centre of a town or on the farm. I would not suggest that such a fury of activity is completely unrealistic. I am occasionally reminded of wall pictures I have used in the past when I am driving. A cyclist comes up from the left; three children are playing with a ball at the roadside; Mr Smith, the grocer, is seeing Mrs Green out of his shop; there is a policeman directing a bus and two lorries (a big one and a little one); a postman is delivering; there is a weathervane on the church, a clock on the Gothic town hall and a train in the station. Fortunately, such a concentration of industriousness is rare or life would be too complicated.

In many ways the wall picture is reminiscent of the basic opposition between simple stimulus-response of the type discussed in chapter 4. The wall picture contains too many things for perception to have the same intensity in every corner of it. Inevitably the contents have to be itemised and the events listed. The teacher leads the S-R progression through the picture, with the class taking little part. If all items are of importance to the teaching there are too many of them to enable sufficient valid perception by the student. If only a few of the items are important the rest have no place in the picture.

The illustrations can link the linguistic and teaching points to the total context of situation. Each illustration, relating to a linguistic item, can function also as part of a sequence which adds up to a situation. There is need to present material in two ways: first, linking each to an utterance, then adding the pictures (and utterances) to form a total (audio-) visual situation.

Unlike the strip cartoonist, who may need to make only one point—in the final picture—and who can depend on a high degree of redundancy in the preceding pictures in the strip, the teacher must reckon with the efficiency of his or her teaching at every moment. He or she may occasionally, for revision, or entertainment, use complete sequences of pictures for the primary impact, the total effect. For most of his or her teaching each picture and each detail must have its own full impact.

If the series of pictures is presented at one and the same time the effect is nearly the same as with the wall picture. The human being will try to assess everything within his field of perception. Unless prevented by the method of presentation the student will try to understand the sequence all at once. Without considering the effects of different reading directions (between Chinese and Frenchmen, for instance) on the reading of pictures laid out in series, it is certain that a series of this kind may be perceived as a whole or perceived from any point to any point. To say that the probability of left to right or right to left is high takes no account of the contrariness of human nature or of the tensions of the learning situation. Little more control over the student's perception is possible than was true of the all-in-one picture. The only advantage is that in the case of the picture sequence the spatial and temporal relationships *are* available if the student will treat the sequence in the required way.

The illustration is subject to more control if presented in book form, provided the ratio is that of one picture to a page. When more than one picture is presented on a page the problems previously mentioned arise: there can be no real control over the individual's perception procedure, or speed, nor any control over the interference from surrounding pictures. Some control may be introduced by the use of a windowed card. This assumes that the student will be tenacious enough to keep using the card, adjusting its position precisely from picture to picture. As with all previous methods of presentation, once he loses his place he really is lost and the chances of associating audio and visual material in a unique combination are high! If the material is presented as one picture to a double-page-spread directness of perception is achieved, for there is no interference from any other picture at each presentation. There is also a certain degree of control over speed of progress. Nevertheless, both directness of perception and consistent speed depend on the student's conscious co-operation—not to look at the pictures before or after, not to depart from the pace of the teacher or the recorded material.

The most satisfactory method of presentation is by slide, filmstrip or film, since each provides a sequence of frames or (in the case of film) sub-sequences of frames. Each frame can be presented separately (more difficult, but possible, in the case of film) and thus full control can be kept over each student's perceptual range. They also enable variation in speed, which can be used to work from the frame through the sub-sequence and back to the re-creation of the total situation.

There are many who reject the use of the visual component and prefer to work with audio-lingual material. The objections are many: that language does not exist in terms of pictures, with their implied simplicity of formation; that there is no transfer from pictures to the cold light of real conversation; that pictures fail to convey their meaning unambiguously.

These objections rest largely on the poor quality of much visual material that has been produced, and on the assumption that the visual material is no more than an important temporary support for the language material. Pictures do not need to be obscure; transfer is difficult in any case and presentation is helped by visual accompaniment; at the most elementary level, concepts are those of tangible reality and pictures have an important part to play. As the course advances, situational pictures are less pointed in their references and accumulated 'experience' within the course will have taken over a greater part of 'comprehension'. Nevertheless, even at the most advanced level, visual material can serve to remind the learner of backgrounds, of situational outlines, of gesture and attitude within the target language system.

Before a lesson it is essential to make sure that the equipment is in order and ready for work. Equally important is the lacing of tape or filmstrip, the sequencing of slides, so that the first thing seen or heard by the class will be the first frame of teaching material. Titles and announcements are distracting. Everything should be so arranged that the operation of only one button on each presentation device will start the lesson.

The presentation text will be played through two or three times to familiarise the class with the general outlines of the situation. No comment from teacher or students is necessary. The run-throughs should be intensive, broken only by the short time necessary to return the material to the start after each.

Here is a short text for audio-visual (or audio-lingual) presentation and some suggestions for working with it. The general pattern of presentation is taken to be that described in the teacher's handbook of the *Voix et Images de France* course (Harrap; published in France by Didier). It is, of course, impossible to anticipate the very special circumstances which may attend one class. One objection which most teachers will raise can, however, be anticipated and answered. No student will persist with demands for an 'explanation' (by which he means a grammatical explanation in traditional terms or translation) if the teacher shows confidence in the material (and offers no explanations), if the material is interesting, if the equipment functions well at normal class sessions. If a high intensity is maintained there will be no opportunity for explanations to be given except in the well-earned coffee-break, by which time every member of the class will almost certainly believe that progress is being achieved anyway.

(1) CHARLES: Georges, vous avez bien regardé l'entrée?
(2) GEORGES: Oui, le concierge a ouvert la grand'porte
(3) à six heures.
(4) Puis il a balayé le vestibule.
(5) CHARLES: Il est resté là
(6) à balayer
(7) jusqu'à quelle heure?
(8) GEORGES: Il a balayé le vestibule et le perron
(9) pendant une demi-heure;
(10) oui, cela a duré bien trente minutes.
(11) CHARLES: Puis il est rentré, je suppose?
(12) GEORGES: Non, il est sorti tout de suite,
(13) il a failli courir.
(14) CHARLES: Est-ce qu'il a couru?
(15) GEORGES: Non, comme je l'ai dit, il a marché vite,
(16) il a failli courir,
(17) mais il est vraiment trop vieux
(18) pour faire l'athlète.
(19) CHARLES: Alors, il a quitté le bâtiment.
(20) Vous savez où il est allé?
(21) GEORGES: Non, il n'est pas revenu.
(22) CHARLES: Quoi!
(23) Vous dites qu'il n'est pas rentré?
(24) GEORGES: Il n'y a pas de concierge à présent.
(25) Il n'y a pas de surveillance.
(26) L'heure H est arrivée.
(27) CHARLES: D'accord.
(28) Ce soir.
(29) A l'œuvre.

Two run-throughs may be enough. Whether this is so or not will depend on the class, the material, the weather... The teacher's decision will depend on whether the outline of progress within the situation has been perceived by the class: this a demand on the teacher's intuition. During the run-throughs, of course, there is no need for the teacher to stand passively by. His or her reactions to the material will encourage the class to react and to perceive more actively. Comprehension of the *total* situation must take place and the material must be presented in the same way as often as necessary until this has been achieved. There should be no difficulty in achieving this unless the material is hopeless!

The second run-through should be slow and careful, making

the class and individuals within it take over the commentary, making the taped material comparatively insignificant. Indeed it is possible to display the visual, ask a question or make a statement to be contradicted with the appropriate utterance, and at the same time play the tape. In this way the taped response is heard but is dominated by the class responses.

The object is to make the taped material completely unnecessary. If the course is an audio-lingual one the taped material will by this stage have been memorised; if audio-visual, the visual material will offer a support to recall at this stage. In any case, the class must be taken through the unit again until the taped material is truly superfluous. In the process some of the frames and utterances will become linked.

In departing occasionally from the original and reminding the class of the appropriateness of material already known, the support of the visual material is gradually reduced. It should, in fact, by now be largely dispensable.

The class is now called on to speak a commentary on the situation which has been put before them. Prompts should be given in the foreign language.

STUDENT: 'Georges a regardé l'entrée'
STUDENT: 'Il a vu le concierge *ouvert la grand'porte'
TEACHER: 'Il a vu le concierge ouvrir la grand'porte. Qu'est-ce qu'il a vu?'
STUDENT: 'Il a vu le concierge ouvrir la grand'porte'
STUDENT: 'Il a vu comme le concierge a ouvert la grand'porte'
TEACHER: 'A quelle heure...?'

Some considerable time may be spent in building up a number of alternative commentaries and in freeing the class from close reliance on the original situation, while retaining the vocabulary and grammar.

TEACHER: 'Il a couru comme un athlète pour prendre l'autobus'
STUDENT: 'Non, il a failli courir mais l'autobus est parti trop vite'
TEACHER: 'A quelle heure est-ce que vous avez quitté votre appartement?'
STUDENT: 'A neuf heures'
TEACHER: 'Vous avez marché vite!'
STUDENT: 'Oui, j'ai failli courir'
TEACHER: 'Pourquoi est-ce que vous n'avez pas couru?'
STUDENT: 'Je suis trop fatigué, je travaille trop dur pour faire l'athlète'

In this way the class is gradually led into 'conversation' without realising it and without feeling the need to look for a really worthwhile subject. The distance from the original subject-matter can be increased. The original visuals or those of previous lessons can be used as a basis for fantasy. It is important that everyone should feel free to talk. As always, individual errors should be submerged in the total group and class activity. Whether accurate facts or inaccurate fantasy, no individual in the class should have occasion to feel his contribution is unwelcome. The object should again be to fill the room with the sound of the target language. Occasionally the class may be broken into smaller groups, but only at advanced levels of proficiency.

The teacher's function in the 'conversation', or as it is sometimes more honestly called 'display' session, is to furnish visual or situational material which will allow the class to reproduce, in various combinations, already known units of the target language. Apart from this, his job is to intervene where any member of the class is heading down a blind alley in the language, completing the student's statement or suggesting another way of saying it, and noting the weak point that may have to be dealt with at some time. As in the later stages of the earlier class session, the teacher should be in the background until moments of difficulty arise. He should be taking part as a member of the class, so that intervention will come easily when it becomes necessary to help another member of the class. Any such intervention, moreover, should come swiftly if at all and be submerged by the immediately succeeding and surrounding class activity.

I have described the process so far as though it were purely linear. I have omitted the formal drilling which will accompany most of the stages mentioned and I have talked of only one kind of display session. Work will more or less centre around the presentation material of the course and here is one very good reason for ensuring that material is as relevant to the learners' needs as possible, since it is the subject-matter of the presentation material which must serve as the principal basis of the student's performance at the 'display' stage.

When the group has mixed requirements, it is sometimes possible to have supplementary display sessions prepared for by a highly relevant situation. The acting out of sketches which parallel parts of the presentation situation may be prepared, and complete parallel situations may be presented for further stimulation to performance. If the original presentation text was a dialogue the parallel text might be a narrative of the same events or another dialogue with some of the facts changed.

The display session may be 'free', as described above, or con-

trolled. Purposeful control can be introduced by asking members of
the class to act out well-described or otherwise delimited rôles. The
sketch mentioned earlier might be in terms of rôle-playing rather
than in terms of an external situation. Here, once more, there is
an advantage in relevance throughout the material. Rôle-playing will
be easier where the rôles are familiar and where the previous material
has shown others in similar rôles. Two students might each be given
a short description in the foreign language, such as:

You have arrived at a hotel and you find no reservation for you. It is late.
Persuade the receptionist that it is the hotel's responsibility to accom-
modate you. Are you angry?—or just sad?

*or :*

This man says he has booked a room for the night. The booking system
in your hotel is faultless. You do not believe him. The hotel is full. He
could be fooling you. Be firm but fair. Eventually you will have to make
room for him—or will you?

At least one of the participants here would be in the hotel and
catering trade. If not, there are difficult moments in every human
situation! Brains trusts, debates, committee meetings, press con-
ferences, as well as the more obvious 'Twenty Questions' are useful
means of revising and extending known material, providing that
they follow effective teaching.

The display session activities must be both *relevant* and *within
the abilities and interests* of the participants. If both the professional
requirements and the interests and abilities of a class are mixed,
the rôle-playing will have to be very varied, unless some staggered
system of display sessions is possible.

For young children, rôle-playing is a kind of professional requirement in itself! Clearly the room must be full of objects which
can be touched and used in playing. Visual material is essential,
and it must be clear and to the point frame by frame. For most
primary schoolchildren and a lot of junior secondary schoolchildren, a sequence can never be longer than two or three frames:
(1) Punch raises his stick—(2) the stick hits Judy—(3) Judy screams.
For most children here is one event, (2), preceded and followed by
(1) and (3). There is little awareness of cause and effect. A longer
sequence would consist of groups similarly structured around a few
emotive frames. The increased use of sequenced visual material in
education, particularly of television, will undoubtedly render comprehension more sophisticated, but the language teacher works with
present abilities and must realise these limitations.

The teacher will know just how much attention he or she can expect from the class of young children at any one time. Activities will be of short duration. Poetry and songs can help to extend the language learning into other parts of the day. Many children's games are very 'linguistic' but the foreign language may sometimes play only a small part in the game. Adults and children who speak the target language should be imported into the classroom to enhance the real-world reality of play language.

Reading and writing can be introduced in the way that it is in the native language, by word-recognition, by card games, by dictionary games, later by project work.

The young secondary schoolchild presents peculiar problems. Personality measurement should play a particularly important part in grouping and the planning of study between the ages of 10 and 13. The most suitable approach to work will vary enormously between these ages. It is essential that classes at this stage should be taught by the same teacher and that there should be the fullest discussion and collaboration with any teacher who has been responsible for previous language learning.

A large part of the first year in the secondary school will need to be spent in work similar to the primary school but with more attention to project work. As soon as it is ready the class should be introduced to increasingly intensive audio-visual or audio-lingual material. Here the 'professional' interests felt by the children will probably be for great detail in various specialisations. Films and slides, with accompanying tapes, can be assembled. There is a lack of suitable specialised material on film and tape for language teaching, and teachers will be limited to the general audio-visual and audio-lingual course until suitable material is available. Fortunately there are well-documented and well-illustrated books available in technical and professional aspects of most European countries. These will serve as sources for project assignments.

The extent to which this work is possible in the secondary school will depend on the demands of any secondary examinations. It is probable that some or all of the class time will have to be given over to preparation for the examination. Audio-visual and audio-lingual work will have a relevance to the oral examination and will serve as the basis, through extension to reading and writing, for composition. With it can be associated at least the resultant version of translation into the foreign language (just as some awareness of grammatical English will have a part to play in the translation from the foreign language). Inevitably, however, the vocabulary and grammar covered in any pre-examination course will have less to do with the relevance and interest for the individual than with the probability of occurrence of these items in the examination.

Although there is transfer from speaking and listening proficiency to writing and reading proficiency, the problems of the examination course deserve to be considered separately in view of their importance in the language teaching field. Whatever may be said about language examinations as tests of language proficiency, and however much one looks forward to improvements in the method and content of examinations, they do exist, and occupy many language teachers for much if not all of their time.

The language teacher who recognises his or her responsibility as that of teaching a degree of proficiency in some or all the skills of language as well as ensuring success in the examination will require the audio-visual or audio-lingual course to play an important part in the language teaching. Indeed the carefully prepared course can impose a discipline and an intensity in the teaching which offers a useful basis even when the only concern is with success in the examination.

In the situational approach linguistic items and subject-matter are interwoven. The extension to reading and writing, as we shall see, works from the basic situations of the presentation material. Written narrative and dialogue will come from the regular noting down of oral commentary which will be well-formed because linked to a situation which is well known. An oral commentary on a taped situation, a filmstrip or a set of pictures which has previously served for class work can be paralleled a few weeks later by an oral commentary in English on the same visual or aural material (easier, of course, with 'neutral' visual material). The resultant written commentaries offer a more satisfactory approach to translation than an entirely phrase-for-phrase conversion. In any case, it can serve as a useful corrective against the production of 'accurate' but dead translations. Indeed very often the real-world requirement is for a second-language *summary*, and it is to be hoped that examinations will reflect this need. Existing translation training can be varied by the production of second language summaries of taped or visual material already known well.

The production of written commentaries is training for so-called 'free composition'. Many examinations are now using picture stimuli, and this will clearly relate to audio-visual work. The preservation of parts of filmstrip or slide sequences (frames from the beginning, the middle, the end) will leave the student to compose in order to fill the gaps, but within the bounds of a familiar situation. Gradual fading of the visual stimuli will lead the student to become self-reliant in narrative or dialogue writing in the target language.

It is difficult to see how the dictation test can be prepared for except by working through what regular sound-symbol relationships exist in the language and by extensive reading and writing.

The primary schoolchild learns to read and write in the foreign language in the same way as in the native language. Experience and the motivation of play alone will serve this end.

The secondary schoolchild and the adult will work from the dictation of phrases with regular orthographic notations and the *learning* of common phrases where there is little or no connexion between pronunciation and spelling. The texts dictated should soon begin to relate to situations already known. In this way there can be a merger of composition and dictation work. There should be no need for an examination dictation to include dictation of the punctuation, whatever the level of the examination, if the subject-matter is within the experience and comprehension of the examinee.

It has been suggested that writing, in the case of older children and adult learners, might start from the dictation of phrases with a high proportion of 'regular' spelling. These regular sound-symbol relationships are taught first through their own patterns, and through success in writing down phrases spelt on the same regular pattern. Undoubtedly the linear teaching machine could do much of this work if combined with a tape-recorder. Phrases are dictated in entire units *at native speed* in the foreign language

> il cherche la machine
> /ilʃɛrʃlamaʃin/
>
> il est petit
> /ilɛpti/
>
> je n'ai pas de cigarettes
> /ʒnepadsigaret/

Part of the skill in dealing with dictation outside the usual examination is in handling it at native speed and in introducing punctuation in accordance with one's comprehension of the global meaning.

As writing develops in this way, reading texts should be introduced. They should be short (20–30 words) accounts of situations already known, or parallel dialogues. A large proportion will be phrases already written at that stage. New vocabulary and structures *may* be included but they must be very few and must certainly not block comprehension.

Redundancy has already been used in the presentation text, for there was no insistence on the semantic evaluation of each phrase, simply an assumption of *global* understanding. Within any piece of continuous language there will be several levels of importance for comprehension. The principal points in any narrative, dialogue or argument are unlikely to number more than three. At the next level there will be points in support of the principal points, or events underlining the principal events. In simple structure passages there will be few other levels in support; in dense structure passages there will be numerous ramifications.

Here are three versions of a very short passage by way of illustration. The first has a straightforward, simple structure, and might be considered as conveying one principal item of information. A–E suggest the next level of information; whilst (1)–(9) mark *all* the other information that it is possible to find in it. The second passage covers exactly the same principal item of information. A–E and (1)–(9) refer to the same points of information as before. There is an additional level of detail ((i)–(v)) and already the passage is far more complex, although the structure remains fairly straightforward. Obviously, longer passages might show considerable density of structure within and between paragraphs (that is, generally, between principal points).

### Simple structure vs. denser structure

(1) A In the morning (2) B 200 workers assembled C (3) outside the factory. (4) A van was (5) already there and they were (6) D listening to the (7) E voice coming from (8) the loudspeaker on top of it.

(1) A In the early morning, (i) before the management would have woken (2) B, 200 workers (ii) dressed in a variety of Sunday-best clothing, assembled C (3) outside the (iii) solid, grey-brick factory. (4) A fussy little van was (5) already there and the assembled crowd was (6) D listening (iv) uncertainly (7) E to the voice from (v) the twin horns of the (8) loudspeaker (9) rising from its roof.

(1) A In the very (a) early morning, (i) before the managerial (b) class would have woken, (2) B 200 of the (c) paint assembly shop workers, (ii) dressed in a variety of Sunday best clothing, assembled (d) silently C (3) outside the (iii) solid, grey-brick (e) façade of the (f) pickle factory.

(4) A fussy little (g) American van (5) was already there and the assembled crowd was (6) D listening (iv) with (h) growing uncertainty (7) E to the

(j) rasping voice from the (v) twin horns of the (k) fiendish (8) loudspeaker (9) rising from the van's (l) jaunty roof.

Complexity of detail should be introduced into reading texts, but the questions or resultant discussion should be concerned with only one or two levels of information. With more experience of reading, learners may be presented with two different reading activities— *intensive* and *extensive* reading. As the names imply, *intensive* reading will deal with short reading passages and concentrate attention on several levels of information; *extensive* reading will present a lot of reading material and require attention to only one or two levels. This division of reading activities will be of considerable help to the learner with reference to his own language too. One of the greatest problems facing the student in any form of higher education is the amount of extensive reading to be done. He is usually only prepared for detailed (intensive) reading.

Any preparation for writing in the foreign language must be based on pattern drilling (and I shall be dealing with this in a later chapter) and this must obviously be based on an analysis of the patterns of orthography in the language. Where written forms are very different and need to be treated as lexical items in themselves (as in Chinese) the activity of reading and writing must be treated separately from the spoken language. Where the script is different but in a reasonably clear relationship to the phonemic aspects of the phonology, as in Russian or Arabic, the teaching of orthographic patterns is fairly simple. Where the language uses entirely roman script there will be considerable difficulty in dissociating the shapes from the prejudices of the native language. Speakers of English find little difficulty with European languages when they have been brought to realise that in few of those languages does the relationship between orthography and pronunciation operate at less than word size, as it does so often in English (there is no other way of dealing with such inconsistences as 'meat'/'great'; 'think'/'then').

Drilling runs parallel to all the activities I have described, and particularly to the audio-visual and audio-lingual procedures I described earlier in this chapter.

At all stages there must be drilling in formal aspects of the language. The most suitable equipment for this procedure is the language laboratory, but a tape-recorder or the lone teacher can carry it out, although with less intensity. General principles and methods of drill design will be dealt with in the chapter on material. It is important to remember, however, that drilling is complementary to all other work and must be seen to be related to that work. For this reason it is wrong to have a separate teacher for the language laboratory. For this reason, too, it is best to start each drill off with items which relate in content to the situations and texts of the relevant unit.

At a very delicate level of work this may not be possible, since the semantic content may be insignificant. This applies particularly to some pronunciation drilling. There is considerable discussion about the extent to which pronunciation should be drilled alone. In an ideal course a very delicate level of pronunciation training would be desirable and some discrimination training might well precede the course. However, where time is limited, as it always is, certain priorities have to be established. In a course which treats the spoken language as central to language learning, any work with lexis or grammar will involve the student in operations with the phonology of the foreign language. A lot of pronunciation drilling could take place without much attention to grammatical or lexical aspects. Indeed, the greater the delicacy of pronunciation work the nearer it comes to acoustic phonetics and the less it has to do with linguistic systems. The allophone is far less essential than the allomorph.

At the advanced levels of a language course the emphasis will in most cases move over to the written language. Intensive reading will play a greater part, having been prepared by a gradual increase in the levels of complexity dealt with. Writing may begin to have stylistic concern, within the limits of the student's natural ability. There will be some training in the linguistic items characteristic of one or two registers of the language. Revision of grammatical items will be needed occasionally and there will be occasion for closer work on sound contrasts. More than ever, though, the language will be used as a tool for further investigation of the foreign country and its way of life. The study of modern literature will be one of the ways to this end and will be complemented by the study of the modern theatre, politics, religion, economics—in the foreign language.

Any study of the literature, theatre, film, radio, publicity will be studying areas where verbal harmonics and semi-grammatical language play an important part. At this stage a basic course on the linguistic structure of the language would be valuable as a preliminary to such study.

'Error'-sensitivity, like the frown, is the characteristic of the teacher. In many subjects error is the opposite of correctness, a binary opposition which presents few difficulties: Sydney is in

Australia—true; York is in Southern England—false. In the humanities any such treatment is too insensitive and yet it has been the normal approach. There is in language a whole range of error—from the educated, native 'solecism' to the foreign language calque.

It is for the teacher to decide on his priorities, with the aid of linguistic description and his realisation of what is possible. He must realise that dealing with error in bulk will help no-one except the statistician. The following is a very short example of the kind of work which a teacher might receive. Numbers are shown at points where most teachers would consider an error to have occurred. Many teachers would give the same value to all the errors and each would probably receive the same intensity of red pencil. In fact so much correction would be written in that the result would be meaningless to the student, if not indecipherable. Yet of the eight or nine errors only three are in reality so serious as to need emergency treatment. Moreover, it is likely that these errors are the ones common to many students. The diffuseness which usually prevents a teacher learning from his students' mistakes comes from a failure to assess error with any delicacy.

<sup>(1)</sup>

Un jour quand M. Truffaut avais une vacance il sorta et alla à voir son
tante qui habita dans la campagne.

Marked are errors as they would normally be judged in school marking. Each error marked would count as one point, ∴ 9. The errors can be classified as follows:

(1) Slight error of collocation, but an error which could be made by anyone, say after a hesitation. MINOR ERROR
(2) 'S' for 't'—slip of pen? Graphological error only. Morpheme recognition still possible. MINOR ERROR
(3) Complete calque of English. GROSS ERROR
(4) Misclassification of common verb. GROSS ERROR
(5) Complete calque of English. GROSS ERROR
(6) Uncommon but not unacceptable French. MINOR ERROR
(7) Root morpheme 's'. Affixal morpheme binary choice. In any case not significant with this lexical item. MINOR ERROR
(8) The contrast imperfect/past definite is not formal (meaningful) but essentially stylistic. MINOR ERROR
(9) Quite acceptable in French. NO ERROR

The result is five minor errors, three gross errors. Group (4) (5) (6) contains two gross errors and could be remedied as *one* unit within the system of French.

For the learner there are a number of broad types of error possibility:

mis-selection of a lexical item (vocabulary);
misformation of a formal pattern (grammar);
misformation of a phoneme (pronunciation);
mis-selection of a stress or intonation pattern (pronunciation).

For three good reasons the teacher should ignore the occasional error:

(*a*) If he or she does not the learners will become inhibited (and if no-one speaks no-one makes errors).

(*b*) With one or two exceptions redundancy operates to make the single error less important than the acceptable total. The exceptions are: the selection of certain lexical items which might block communication or give offence to the native listener; selection of a formal pattern which gives the wrong message to the native listener (factual or social), for instance in languages with morphological or other distinctions of politeness; the consistent selection of an intonational pattern which might block communication or signal the wrong social relationship.

(*c*) Practice is better than exhortation and the course material, if well-prepared, will deal with it.

Deviations from what is acceptable will have been dealt with, as suggested, at all stages. In the display session the teacher will lead the student away from the linguistic blind alley. When the student persists in making an error on material which should be within his competence the teacher can use the information to produce remedial texts or drills to supplement the existing course material.

## 6. TESTING

Mettez au parfait: (*a*) Je mets mon chapeau. (*b*) Nous entendons. (*c*) Paul a un livre. (*d*) Cécile mange du pain. (*e*) Elles font leur devoir.

This example of an exercise, typical of most existing textbook courses, is not a teaching mechanism but a test. We shall be considering in the next chapter the principles underlying teaching material. The exercise quoted, like millions of others in daily use, offends one of the principal criteria: there is no pattern, the items are assembled in a completely random order.

If the exercise does not teach, then perhaps it tests? This it does because only already well-learnt material would enable the student to deal successfully with it. It would serve to show the teacher gaps in each student's knowledge. The results from a class would show a complex of error types which would be meaningless for future teaching; alternatively, there might be no errors, the previous work having been well learnt, in which case the all-round success would be equally meaningless since the exercise is neither a reliable sample of learning of the 'passé composé' nor has it relevance to any activity which can now be carried out—apart from the successful completion of this particular test!

The design of any part of the teaching process must be preceded by a thorough description of aims, and of methods which will lead to the achievement of those aims. Tests are no exception. For long tests were regarded as outside teaching, as the antithesis of teaching and it is in this light that one would describe the exercise quoted above, and all those like it, as a test.

One of the most important changes in attitude has been the realisation that tests can play a part in teaching. Many teaching machine programmes must use tests frequently within the teaching material in an attempt to ensure that no student proceeds to material for which he is not prepared. Obviously such tests will be testing specific knowledge or behaviour, will be short, and will be entirely relevant to the next frames of information. In these circumstances a discipline is imposed on the design of the tests by the nature of the information required and its purpose.

Paradoxically, the test in its new function is often scarcely distinguishable from the teaching material. In the teaching programme the only clue to its existence may be its position at a critical point, where a new sub-topic is about to be introduced, or at the point of divergence of a branch or spur.

Fundamental to the behavioural view of learning is a situation shared by testing and teaching:

$$
\begin{array}{ll}
\text{S} & - \qquad\qquad \text{R} \\
\text{Stimulus} & - \text{ response?} \\
& - \text{ response?} \\
& - \text{ (correct) RESPONSE} - \\
& \text{reinforcement} - \text{RESPONSE}
\end{array}
$$

(S) I worked there for 10
             years   —   You still work there (*a*)
                  —   10 years ago (*b*)
                  —   (correct) You don't work
                      there now — .... —

As a teaching item it would include *only* the third (correct) response and would add a number of similar S – R items to bring out the regularity of the pattern. As a test item it is clearly probing the student's ability to distinguish the most appropriate response at sentence level, setting the degree of difficulty by complete contrast (response (*a*)) and by distraction (response (*b*)).

The course material designer also wants to know where to begin, what previous knowledge he may take for granted, what abilities he may rely on. Subsequently he wants to know how successful his course is in achieving the desired 'terminal behaviour'.

For language teaching purposes tests may be considered as having three main functions. In each function they may be concerned with the individual student alone or with him in relation to a particular course. These tests may be used before or at the beginning of a course, within a course, and after or at the end of a course. There is some confusion about the names of these tests but I shall call them, respectively, *prognostic/aptitude*, *diagnostic/indicator*, and *proficiency/achievement* tests.

The prognostic/aptitude test is seldom used, probably because there is rarely a choice of student or a choice of language course open. The prognostic test could be used to establish a profile of an individual's abilities and would serve as a useful guide to the most probable areas of weakness in language learning, suggesting general areas of need for remedial material. The aptitude test measures the individual's abilities in relation to a particular course. It can suggest specific areas of weakness and serve as a preliminary warning of remedial drills that will be needed. In addition it offers a preliminary standard with which the final measure of achievement may be compared, given a wide sample of students, in establishing the efficiency of a course.

The diagnostic test must be very efficient indeed, testing very quickly what has been learnt over a period of time. It can measure the extent to which any individual student is controlling the material at any point. It can be used at critical points within the course when the individual's error rate is significantly higher than the rest of the group. The indicator test is applicable to the group and its progress through the course. In a linear programme it will suggest the next point for each individual to work from, proceeding as before, going back, or jumping ahead. In a branched programme it will tell the individual student whether to proceed as before or what branch to take. In an adaptive programme the indicator test will be even more firmly integrated in the course and the operations of the presentation device.

The proficiency test is not related to any particular course. It is, however, related to a job description and a skill description and these, in their turn, are presumably relevant to the 'terminal behaviour' which is the aim of the selected course. In many ways the proficiency test comes close to the achievement test. The latter, however, measures the student's success in terms of the course. It comes nearest to the examination because it is not primarily related to language skill but to an educational or learning activity.

The prognostic test may measure some or all of the following skills and aptitudes. The aptitude test will consider only those items which relate to the content of the course which the student is about to begin.

A. visual perception
   aural perception
   reading speed
   writing speed
   fluency

B. rote and immediate memory
   aural comprehension
   visual comprehension
   reasoning ability

C. verbal intelligence
   sense of structure

Visual perception may be tested by means of minimally contrastive pictures of the kind often found on the puzzle pages of children's comics. In the aptitude test the picture might relate to a minimal contrast within the course material. The aptitude test could also include a test of graphemic perception related to the language to be learnt, e.g. Russian талый/шалый.

Aural perception may be measured by minimal contrastive sounds in the native language or in the language to be learnt: pride/bride; langue/longue.

Reading and writing speeds in the native language may be timed. A further check will be necessary with the former activity to ensure that reading actually takes place. This can be done by asking the student to mark nonsense words, inappropriate words or certain letters in the text. Fluency in the native language can be timed by the number of words spoken (with due regard to sense) per minute over three minutes, a percentage score being deducted for each break or hesitation. These very individual characteristics might be measured for the sake of completeness. It would be interesting to note if any improvements took place as the result of the subsequent language learning, but these would have educational rather than linguistic implications. Weakness in visual or aural perception might suggest supplementary training before an audio-visual or audio-lingual course. On the whole, however, it is unlikely that measurement of these factors, innate rather than learnt, could be justified as the primary object of prognostic/aptitude testing.

Rote and immediate memory can be tested by the presentation of both meaningful utterances and nonsense syllables. The aptitude test may also include words and syllables from the language to be studied.

Aural comprehension may be tested by calling for an interpretation of meaningful sounds (ah! oh! brr!) and meaningless noises. A picture in which the central event is obscure could be another medium of testing. The student could be asked to state what the event is or to say what the subsequent event will be.

There are well-established tests of reasoning ability, and verbal intelligence can be tested easily ('black is to white as bad is to —'). Testing a sense of structure in the native language is testing an extension of this verbal intelligence.

ONE of these sentences is built in the same way, Which is it?

*The two men entered the room together*

(a) Cut off from land their worst enemy was the weather.
(b) Of their last hours little is known.
(c) Those quiet towns defended their freedom with honour.
(d) Many sudden noises startled the crowd intensely.
(e) Further thought was rendered impossible by Charlie's arrival.

The diagnostic test and indicator test will vary as widely as the linguistic items within the course. The items selected for testing, however, will be principally from these levels of language:

Phonology
Morphology
Syntax

Tests will also be concerned occasionally with the student's performance or competence in dealing with the relevance or appropriateness of linguistic forms to situation (lexis/meaning).

Discrimination of minimal phonological contrasts can be tested with items from the target language: 'La dame aux cheveux blancs/la dame aux cheveux blonds; j'en ai peu/j'en ai peur.' The student can be called on to characterise different intonations as 'anger', 'surprise'. He can be called on to repeat a sound or an utterance, but this brings in difficulties of human measurement which will be my concern later in this chapter.

Morphological discrimination can be tested by asking the student to select the more acceptable of:

(a) er hat das mir in die Fabrik gebracht
(b) er hat das mir in die Fabrik gebrochen

Syntax may be measured by asking the student to combine:

Ich weiss nicht. Ist er ja so klug?

or to select the more appropriate subsequent statement to:

I'll have it rebuilt
(a) Someone else will rebuild it.
(b) I'll rebuild it.

Soon I'll have found it
(a) Someone else will find it.
(b) I'll find it.

Tests of the recognition of appropriate response utterances may be used to test phonological, grammatical and lexical 'meaning'.

Tu veux du café?
(a) Oui, j'ai faim.
(b) Oui, j'ai soif.
(c) Oui, j'aime les restaurants.

I ,was "wanting to ,come
(a) I'm 'sorry ,you 'can't.
(b) I'm 'sorry you 'couldn't.

(In the last item the uninitiated reader will have to 'understand' the intonation marking on the basis that (a) is taken to be the most appropriate response!) Clearly the items would relate to the content of the course, both linguistically and situationally. Much fuller test items would be possible, reports of events previously known, deductions from earlier situational content of the course.

It will be seen that the student is given a choice of 'answer' items ('multiple choice') rather than being asked to compose answers at random. This enables scoring to be more mechanical, important where the material will be used to direct the student immediately to the next work. It also ensures that the student is being assessed only on his handling of the test item, not on his ability to compose responses (writing ability). In what language should the multiple choice responses be? If in the native language is there not an element of translation in the test? If in the target language, the student's aural or reading comprehension is being further tested when he selects the best response. This problem is marginal in the case of diagnostic/indicator tests, since measurement is only directed to improvement in the learning process. The responses must be in the target language unless a very precise diagnosis is required. In the proficiency/achievement test this problem assumes a rather greater importance.

The proficiency/achievement test is concerned less with linguistic items than with their combined use in practical situations. This is not a view that would necessarily be accepted by many workers in the language testing field. There is, indeed, an argument which runs through much discussion of testing and which might be summed up as follows: should the test concern itself with items or with global skills?

There can be little doubt that prognostic and diagnostic tests should concern themselves with the manipulation of items, as illustrated earlier in this chapter. Some of the indicator tests, however, will begin to concern themselves, as the course proceeds, with comprehension (and, occasionally, production) of language items in larger contexts, since the language course must be leading towards greater degrees of delicacy in dealing with larger situational contexts. Since the proficiency test is concerned with global performance the measurement must be of global skill.

Many phonemic and grammatical distinctions at word, clause or sentence level cease to be of importance in the larger context. 't' (/t/) and 'th' (/ð/) represent a phonemic distinction in English; 'letter' and 'leather' are distinguished by this contrast alone; yet 'here's a letter for you' is situationally quite different from 'here's a leather for you' (although distinguished still by only one phoneme). 'Here's a letter for you to read' is no more likely to be confused with 'Here's a leather for you to wash the car with' than is 'Here's a leather for you to read' with 'Here's a letter for you to wash the car with'. Communication is not blocked by the confusion of phonemes—one is possible (in context) as an Anglo-Irish allophone, the other could be a momentary aberration. The phonemic distinction so important at one stage becomes less and less important as the context increases to paragraph and beyond. Redundancy plays such a large part in communication that it should be included in any measurement of proficiency.

The main objections to situational testing are stated by Robert Lado in *Language Testing* (pages 26–7):

The situations in which language is the medium of communication are potentially almost infinite. No one, not even the most learned, can speak and understand his native language in any and all the situations in which it can be used

and

We have no assurance that we have tested language merely because a situation has been understood. And we have no assurance that it is lack of knowledge of the language when a situation is not understood.

This argument overlooks the fact that a proficiency test is in fact asked to test first the ability to understand and take part in a situation and only secondarily (if at all) the use of language for its own sake. It is easy to imagine a student who did very well in item tests being unable to co-ordinate his ability sufficiently to carry out any activity in the language. A valid comparison is that of car driving: the ability to steer, to use the brake does not give any assurance of the co-ordinated use of these things to drive the car; nor does the ability to move the car give an assurance of smooth, safe progress through a town. Similarly, accuracy in dealing with the elements of language does not ensure proficiency in using an integrated skill in the language, and the latter gives no assurance of the ability to carry out a task, to achieve a purpose in the foreign language.

An analysis by activities of proficiency in language suggests the following scheme:

### I. SPEAKING

A. *Sustained speech*

(i) *In a situation, depicted or real*
$S$timulus situational (i.e. non-linguistic) — $R$esponse spoken;
S Non-linguistic — R Foreign language ($L_2$)

(ii) *Oral account of something written*
$S_{written}$ — $R_{spoken}$
S Native language ($L_1$) or $L_2$

(iii) *Argument or counter-statement in answer to statement*
$S_{spoken}$ — $R_s$
S $L_1$ or $L_2$ — R $L_2$

B. *Conversation*

(i) *In a situation, depicted or real*
$$S_{sit} - R_s$$
S Non-linguistic $- R L_2$

(ii) *Discussion of something written*
$$S_w - R_s$$
S $L_1$ or $L_2 - R L_2$

(iii) *Diffuse conversation (dialogue)*
$$S_o - R_s$$
S $L_2 - R L_2$

## 2. AURAL COMPREHENSION (LISTENING)

(i) *Resultant activity*
$$S_s - R_{sit}$$
S $L_2 - R$ Non-linguistic

(ii) *Written summary*
$$S_s - R_w$$
S $L_2 - R L_1$ or $L_2$

(iii) *Oral summary*
$$S_s - R_i$$
S $L_2 - R L_1$ or $L_2$

(iv) *Answer questions*
   (*a*) Constructed response $S_s - R_{s \text{ or } w}$ $\left.\rule{0pt}{14pt}\right\}$ $SL_2 - R L_1$ or $L_2$
   (*b*) Multiple choice       $S_s - R_{choice}$

## 3. WRITING

(i) *In a situation, depicted or real*
$$S_{sit} - R_w$$
S Non-linguistic $- R L_2$

(ii) *Linking of notes to complete a narrative*
$$S_w - R_w$$
S $L_2 - R L_2$

(iii) *Criticism, essay (based on written text)*
$$S_w - R_w$$
S $L_2 - R L_2$

(iv) *Summary of speech, description, narrative*
$$S_s - R_w$$
S $L_2 - R L_2$

## 4. READING

(i) *Resultant activity*
$$S_w - R_{sit}$$
S $L_2 - R$ Non-linguistic

(ii) *Written summary*
$S_w - R_w$
$S\ L_2 - R\ L_1\ or\ L_2$

(iii) *Oral summary*
$S_w - R_s$
$S\ L_2 - R\ L_1\ or\ L_2$

(iv) *Answer questions*
    (*a*) Constructed response $S_w - R_{s\ or\ w}$ $\Big\}$ $S\ L_2 - R\ L_1\ or\ L_2$
    (*b*) Multiple choice       $S_w - R_{choice}$

This is the range of activities constituting communication and which might be included in an ideal battery of proficiency tests. An ideal achievement test battery would include those of the activities relevant to the course. A purely audio-lingual or audio-visual course would prepare for activity-groups 1 and 2; another battery of course-tests might measure an assortment of specific activities taken from various classes as listed above.

Some of the activities listed may have to be omitted from any list of test activities drawn up on the basis of practicability. This does not mean that they may not be practicable at some future stage, nor does it mean that they might not be included, with all their present shortcomings, if the purpose of the language learning demanded such a measurement.

The activity listed as (i) in the groups set out above presents certain difficulties. The main difficulty is that of arranging a situation which will provoke a performance from the testee and yet one which will be delimited sufficiently to ensure consistency of test conditions from one candidate to the next. As a result the relationship between stimulus (S) and performance (R) is not likely to be close enough to be satisfactory. In 3 and 4 instructions (oral or written) might be given which would lead to some set of actions being carried out by the candidate. Clearly this resultant activity might vary enormously unless the $S - R$ (e.g. instructions – action) relationship were part of the training associated with the particular language proficiency requirement. There are obvious instances, such as with airline or ship personnel, where the need to measure performance in response to a situation would be such, and the realistic situation so easy to stage, that other considerations would take second place.

There is, of course, one non-linguistic stimulus to foreign language writing (3 (i)), the picture or set of pictures, which is increasingly frequent in first examination papers. Unlike other non-linguistic stimuli, the picture can offer 'notes' on the subject-matter, and in the same texture as the required response—graphic to graphic—in a way impossible where the required response is phonic.

The oral response of 2 (iii) and 4 (iii) offers no advantage over the written response (2 (ii) and 4 (ii)). To obtain recordings rather than written answers is always going to be difficult and there is no point in seeking difficulties where no advantage exists. For the same reason written composed response answers to 2 (iv) and 4 (iv) would be preferable.

As we shall see, writing is the most difficult activity to assess. Activity 3 (iii), the writing of an essay or criticism in response to something written, is very specialised and can be satisfactory only at an advanced level of language proficiency. It has no place in any test of general proficiency and will rarely have a place outside tests of highly specialised proficiency: literary journalism, literary study, abstract/summary writing. Activity 3 (iv) would place considerable emphasis on the testee's aural comprehension, which is not the subject of the test. Once again, however, it might be included if proficiency in composing a summary of a passage of sustained speech in the foreign language were specifically required.

In many of the activities the stimulus (in group 1) or the response (in groups 2 and 4) may be in the native language ($L_1$) or the foreign language ($L_2$). If $L_1$ is used, some element of translation must occur, and this may be an activity that the teaching has simply not included. If $L_2$ is used, a further minute test of comprehension (where used for the stimulus) or production is being given. In groups 2 and 4 production can be well limited if a choice of answers is given ('multiple choice').

It would be impossible to specify exhaustively the activities in which language proficiency might be measured without analysing all the total activities in which language would play a part. These might include explaining instructions, giving advice, selling (1 A), lecture note taking, receiving instructions or advice, writing telephone message (2), expanding telegrams or writing telegrams (3). Activity tests would always consist of mixtures of the 'purified' activities set out in the schema above, and, as such, would be amenable to the principles of design and assessment set forth here.

The full proficiency test should be preceded by a job description; the achievement test by a course description. This description affects not only the activity or situational content of each test but the linguistic inventory of each skill. Such an inventory, in terms of grammar and lexis, is easier for the achievement test since the attendant course itself provides the details. The establishment of inventories for job-proficiency would provide a feedback of use to designers of specialised courses. Such inventories can be expected as part of the growing work on the analysis of registers and styles of language.

Situational and linguistic content are factors which can be defined in ways already suggested. Another set of variables is provided by the nature of the activity, the length, the time, the blocks set within it.

In sustained speech (group 1) these variables would include the length of time for which the candidate was expected to talk; the amount of preparation-time given; the nature of the written or spoken stimulus (time, length, content). In conversation (group 1) variation of conditions would be limited but less subject to test control. However, controllable variations ('variables') would be the length of the conversation, interruptions, and changes of subject initiated by the examiner. It should be remembered that the examiner is likely to be speaking during half of a normal conversation so that he *can*, in practice, exercise considerable control over the progress of the test.

Variables in the aural comprehension text are again length and timing. The text may be narrative, soliloquy or duologue, the last being the most useful. An example of structure density variation has been given in chapter 5. Blocks to comprehension may be introduced by the inclusion of inconsequences or illogicalities. The test questions may ask for information explicitly given or for deductions to be made about implicit information. This is another factor which will act as variable *within the test* rather than, as would normally be assumed, *within the assessment*.

## A. TELEPHONE CALLS

(*a*) Hallo...hallo...(*sotto voce*) stop it...Mrs Jane Mantle here... That's the Hotel Mirabellois is it? Good...(*drop in volume*) Put it on the top shelf...Will you tell my son-in-law...He's staying there...(*drop in volume*) No, not there, idiot...His cousin Jack's in trouble...He might have to come home...I'll ring again tomorrow at 6 (*drop in volume*) No, lower than that...No, I'd better say twenty to seven otherwise he won't be there...He *could* ring *me*, of course...(*drop in volume*) Leave it then ...I can't ring again tonight, I'll be over at Jack's...If he rings me he'd better try the shop—L E R 7 6 5 1 and do it before 11 in the morning...

(*b*) Hullo...I want to leave a message for Mr Henry Mortello, he's staying there at the moment. I'll be coming on the 10.40 from Paddington ...I don't know what time it gets there tomorrow. Will he arrange for a taxi, and I'll need some lunch. Then if he could lay on the people he wrote to me about I'll see them after lunch, or over lunch if he knows a respectable place...

### B. LECTURE WITH AMBIGUITY

The literary productions of Thomasina have long been neglected by historians but they are probably the best source of contemporary views on the political movements of the 1920s. Beneath the surface of undiluted sentiment there can be detected the reflection of a genius of her time. She was not a great writer, she had no gifts apart from a determination to use green ink and to cover as many pages as possible each day. Around her events of world-shattering importance were taking place. She was insensitive to them, indeed that greenish-grey scrawl filling sheets of paper of every conceivable size and shape seems almost to present a shutter to the world of reality. But below that surface, in the nature of her characters, in their positioning throughout what might in any other writer be called the plot, their positioning in that ooze of sentiment, there are clues for the perceptive reader...

$\equiv$ ambiguity
= consistent unwinding of argument
— apparent contradictions

### C

There were 200 passengers on the boat. The weather had been outstandingly beautiful and the cruise was proceeding smoothly.

The boat was a two-funnelled liner of some...tons, equipped with radar of the very latest design...Along its sides hung the eight lifeboats which gave reassurance to any passenger inclined to be nervous. The lifeboats were a brilliant white in the sunshine. They were large boats, capable of holding twenty persons and enough provisions for a month at sea...

1. There were
    (*a*) 200 passengers
    (*b*) 200 patternmakers
    (*c*) 20 panthers
2. There were
    (*a*) eight lightboats
    (*b*) eighteen lightboats
    (*c*) eight lifeboats
3. The boats were
    (*a*) blue
    (*b*) red
    (*c*) white

4. The boats could hold
   - (*a*) all the passengers
   - (*b*) some of the passengers
   - (*c*) all the passengers and crew

Examples of realistic texts showing the variables which can be introduced:

A. Telephone calls (*a*) and (*b*) clearly differ greatly in complexity.
B. The lecture contains various blocks to comprehension.
C. The questions on this narrative call for comprehension of explicit and implicit facts. Questions 1, 2 and 3 ask for information explicit in the text; question 4 asks for information which must be deduced from other facts.

Clearly, too, the pictures and notes acting as stimuli to writing (3 (i) and (ii)) can be used to vary the test conditions, as will the length expected and the time available. The information content of the notes and pictures is variable.

Realism offers numerous suggestions for variables which may legitimately be used in test design. A telephone message may be hampered by a poor line or (particularly good for hotel receptionists) by a scatter-brained informant; a lecture may contain ambiguities which are clarified by later remarks.

An acceptance of the need for global rather than item-tests places a premium on the methods and criteria of assessment if there is to be any claim to objectivity of scoring. Item-tests are designed not only for delicacy of measurement at phonemic or morphemic level but also to ensure ease of scoring. The assessment of item tests is in most cases amenable to mechanised scoring. The global test, on the other hand, is designed to measure a total activity at a much higher level than the phoneme/morpheme. Inevitably the resultant performance is composed of a number of linguistic and skill factors which must be scored but which are not as yet amenable to mechanical assessment on the same scale. Some human scoring will always be necessary in global language tests.

Speaking ('oral production') (activity group 1) involves the following partial language skills:

> pronunciation
> fluency
> grammar
> lexis

The constituents of *pronunciation* can be assessed separately. One constituent alone may be assessed—say intonation or stress. One testing technique, indeed, is to assess the production of *one* phoneme or *one* intonation pattern whenever it occurs in the total performance. A global assessment can be made on a five-point grading scale related to total phonological performance. The five grades are: near-native, pleasant, acceptable, communicating, non-communicating. It is possible to establish descriptions or to provide taped examples of performance at each grade.

*Fluency* is essentially the measurement of the average rate of ' slow colloquial' speech. Slower or faster rates might be set as other levels of proficiency, although it is reasonable, in normal circumstances, to expect anyone claiming any sort of proficiency in the language to average no less than 150/175 words per minute. Ability to recognise various speeds is easy to acquire. From the maximum score thus established, a deduction of, say, 10 per cent would be made for each serious break in continuity or interest noted by the assessor.

A variety of *grammatical* structures and *lexical* items would be expected within the limits of the course or the proficiency claimed. Deductions would be made for unnecessary repetition and for any inappropriateness of structures or vocabulary used.

In a global test there is an extra element which might be assessed. This is the achievement of the *task*. In activities 1 B (ii) and 1 B (iii) it would be simply the maintenance of a normal discussion or conversation, the exchange of communication in a pleasant way. In 1 A (iii) the task would be achieved by a convincing argument for or against the proposal. In 1 A (ii) the assessment would be of the accuracy of the account.

Aural comprehension testing makes little demand on the assessor, more on the text-writer. 2 (ii), the written summary, will measure the accuracy with which explicit (and implicit) points are reproduced. There is no reason to take account of any other feature of the response activity, since the emphasis is on the action of the stimulus text. Viewed in this light there is little advantage in a written summary over multiple choice response. The latter can be scored purely on a 1 : 1 basis. The use of multiple choice response in activity 4 (iv), also enables the scoring to be greatly simplified.

Writing is certainly the most difficult skill to assess objectively. The proficiency/achievement test concerns itself rarely with stylistic writing for its own sake, and the subjective element in assessment can be discounted to a large extent because of the functional nature of the writing activity. In addition to linguistic variety and accuracy does the student's performance achieve the task set?

In some languages the accuracy of the candidate's *graphology* (script) needs to be measured and a score then attached to the measurement. *Grammar* and *lexis* are assessed as described earlier. Although the writing may have no consciously stylistic purpose, a score (on a five-point scale similar to that for pronunciation) should be available for an overall impression of the arrangement and assembly of the written text.

It will be seen that subjective aspects of assessment can be reduced or delimited. Combined with the specific description of stimulus and response texts and activities, this offers global testing without the relinquishment of objective test standards.

The achievement test battery and the examination can be very similar but rarely are. They do set out to attain the same end, to establish a measurement of achievement in terms of an actual or notional course. The achievement test is always concerned with an individual's language proficiency, albeit limited to the criteria of skills which guided the test design. Discipline is imposed on both test and course by the application of linguistic criteria and by the close description of relevant activities.

There may be interaction of some kind between the examination (by way of the examining board) and the rather vague aims of the courses at institutions which habitually prepare students for it. Linguistic and functional criteria play a very minor rôle since the language examination must fit into a pattern shared by a range of subjects with nothing in common with language skills. This different, essentially non-linguistic, concern of the examination is one point which distinguishes it from the achievement test. Another is the greater number of candidates to whom it will be administered. The prime aim of an examination conducted on a national scale is to provide valid statistics, and actual results (= scores) will be manipulated to ensure the curve of validity, the 'normal distribution'.

The enormous size of the examination industry in Britain, for instance, has led to a hardening of marking procedures to ensure simplicity and the necessary easy consistency of marking. The tendency has been to encourage activities which are amenable to a 1 : 1 marking scheme or to mark other activities with less concern for the relevance of the marking to the proficiency being measured than for the simplification of marking itself.

There is, of course, no inherent reason why examinations must be set on a large scale. Techniques of sampling of assessment and moderation are sufficiently advanced to justify the design, administration and marking of language (and, indeed, other) examinations

within large schools or between schools in a small area. The English
Certificate of Secondary Education Examination is working on these
lines, and one hopes that it can withstand the doubtful prestige
competition from national and regional examinations. Perhaps some
of these examinations may consider moving in this direction. There
are reasons why they should, but there are also reasons why they
need not. As the sorters of some of the sheep from some of the goats
they do their job reasonably well, with no concern for measuring
proficiency in any subject except by chance. Their prestige comes
less from their validity as measuring instruments than from their
large-scale applicability. This is undoubtedly the main reason why
few language teachers have taken up the option of proposing an
alternative syllabus for their students.

The hesitation in giving oral examinations a larger part to play
in the total examination comes from the (tacitly) recognised unreliability of such examinations at present. The oral examiner receives no training, is given few guide-lines, and no sampling
assessment is carried out by means of tape-recording. Moreover,
it seems unlikely that an increased oral component in these large-
scale examinations will develop without a reduction in the size of
the areas for which they are responsible. Central assessment and
the objective assessment of each individual's performance will depend on a considerable use of tape-recording. The thought of de-
spatching and receiving all those tapes is breathtaking. Written
papers are far easier to handle, of course. However, the amount of
tape handled could be reduced by using sampling techniques to their
fullest advantage, maintaining a mark adjustment coefficient for
each examination centre on the basis of thoroughgoing spot checks.
The amount of tape preparation, copying and handling could be
virtually eliminated if centres (large schools and small areas) were
given responsibility for setting language examinations and assessing
the performance of their students. Preparation for such moves would
include a greater component of training in testing and examining
techniques for student teachers and serving teachers.

Meanwhile the situation changes slowly, if at all. A recent
analysis of examinations held by a number of the British examining
boards showed that practically every one of them called for translation into and from the foreign language; almost all called for a
written composition and all included dictation.

There is no justification for translation at any but the most advanced, nearly bilingual, level of proficiency. It presupposes a
relationship between languages which does not exist at less than

the level of the total language systems. At any lesser level, at phrase, sentence or paragraph level, the differences between the two perceptual grids which reflect and are reflected by the two languages are part of the total set of differences between these two systems. Any attempt to convert one language into another, to see a set of events from the same angle in spite of vast referential, linguistic and social differences, must bend one of the languages. It may work with the language of near-neighbour communities, provided that the text is naïve, but the result of translation will scarcely be more than a calque of the original. Existing marking procedures, too, look for the possibilities of right-wrong judgments at scarcely more than the morphemic level. Translation is an exercise in two cultures, an exercise of style in interpretation, and the assessment of style is notoriously difficult.

Written composition offers similar problems. It can only be done at all if a considerable level of proficiency has been reached. Any such activity at a lower level is likely to be a reproduction of an original from memory or the collection of a number of units of the language, grammatically and lexically correct in themselves, which collectively, at a higher linguistic level, form at best an accurate calque of a half-formed native language composition but have little to do with the foreign language.

Dictation measures a little aural comprehension and a lot of the sound-symbol mechanism (in those languages where it exists). It also measures knowledge of lexical items and their spelling, but the exercise is not intended to test this latter item and the text is rarely chosen on the basis of knowledge to be expected of the student. In many ways the dictation is the best of the three activities mentioned, as a test of a partial skill. Moreover it is amenable to scoring on accuracy alone and can be marked easily and consistently— except when the text is really ambiguous. On the other hand, it has little relationship to any real-life activity.

Many of the functions of the language examination will undoubtedly be superseded by the test, which is a far more accurate measurement if tailored to a well-described set of functional needs. The general educational system may retain the examination for its own purposes. Further education and the professions will turn more and more to tests designed for specialised needs.

# 7. MATERIAL

Whatever the language teacher accepts or rejects of the 'new waves' in linguistics, psychology and pedagogy, some things are certain. The teacher is concerned with the achievement of a certain 'standard' or 'terminal behaviour' in his pupils. The teacher would probably like to use a textbook arranged in a slightly different order, perhaps at a slightly different speed, with more material there and less material here. In other words he wishes the book were better 'programmed'. He may also wish that the physical conditions under which he works were better, he would like soundproofing, lighting and so on.

The textbook he uses probably reaches the 'standard' as specified by the examination or, if he is not dominated by the public examination, by the (often tacit) criteria that he has brought or has caught from the school system in which he was taught himself or now teaches. It is to be hoped that the present book may cause more language teachers to question the nature of these 'standards' and their relationship to language proficiency.

Nothing can be done about the physical conditions except to remind teachers that they *can* gain improvements if they know what they want and why, know their priorities and will speak with one voice to the responsible authorities.

The language teacher is not likely to find a textbook adjusted to his needs. Nor is it likely that course material will be any better until the large-scale courses begin to appear, offering a wealth of parallel texts and remedial drills. This will be a slow development, since the producers of such large-scale material must be sure that the material is indeed relevant to the needs and the problems, not to say the physical conditions, of all potential users.

The combination of audio-visual, audio-lingual and programming techniques results in an amalgam of material which may be broken into and rewritten in a way that textbooks have never offered. Textbooks would have been more useful in the past if they had been provided in a loose-leaf form, allowing material to be omitted or added.

The teacher should be prepared to add written and taped material to whatever course he has adopted. Within his teaching, from class to class even, there are variations in conditions, in interest, in motivation. Future course material may anticipate and deal with these variations but many of them will be at too delicate a level for the general course to deal with. The teacher may produce remedial and revision texts and drills to use these variations in the teaching situation, or he may treat the course, as many have treated the text-book, as something complete to which the learner must be fitted. It is unlikely, however, that the teacher with this kind of respect for the sanctity of what is sent from the publisher or the education office will have continued reading so far into this book.

Inevitably teachers will be consulted more often on the adoption of particular material. It is as much a part of each teacher's pro-fessional responsibility as anything else to demand the best material and to feel competent to supplement or gradually replace material whenever it is found wanting.

*Presentation texts* have four main functions:

(a) to interest;
(b) to provide subject-matter and
(c) linguistic items (mainly lexical) for use during succeeding practice of the grammatical structures;
(d) to show by contrasts, progression within the whole context of the text, the occurrences of the formal pattern—its formal 'meaning'.

A teacher will know the areas of interest of his students. If no specialisation is of concern to them an appeal must be made to more general interest. As any writer of entertainment material knows, 'colour' is important. A neutral text is one weakness from which educational films have often suffered in the past. Whether comic, tragic, mysterious or exasperating, the events must add up to a situation or a narrative which leaves no-one 'cold'. At the same time the units of language presented must be of a kind which will be of use in later lessons and of more general use to the learners.

The precise teaching point will have been defined. For the most part this will be a point of grammar. There are languages where a set of formal phonological changes is necessary in different social situations or to distinguish the sex or age of the speaker. In such languages contrasting situations would carry contrasts in the phono-logical systems. In extreme cases it would be a matter of organising classes so that they were divided on the basis of these sociolinguistic needs, making divisions of sex, age or class according to the dis-tinctions recognised formally in the language.

Purely segmental (or *sub-morphemic*) phonological variations are consistent at only the word level. No context will illustrate or practise the contrast ou/u in French, or any other contrast, at a level higher than the word without artificiality stultifying every part of it. 'rue' /ry/ contrasts with 'roue' /ru/. 'Le duc juge la rue' contrasts with 'Froufrou pousse la roue' less well than 'c'est la rue/ c'est la roue', but the contrast is non-existent at a high (contextual) level of structure. Intonational contrast by its very nature functions at sentence level and higher. Here again, artificiality is impossible to avoid if consistency throughout several sentences is maintained in an area of language where in all but a few specialised registers variety alone is acceptable. Concentration on phonological features is left to drills and will be dealt with in the appropriate section of this chapter.

The text, then, is entirely concerned with grammar and lexis, with emphasis on the former rather than the latter. It has been made clear in a previous chapter that grammar has formal meaning as a result of its structure as a *closed* system. Lexis also has meaning only partly as a result of its existence in collocations. Lexical items belong to open sets and their formal 'meaning' (i.e. their position in the set and their relationship with the other items) is essentially fluid. Precision of 'meaning' is never possible, even in one's native language, unless each term is defined within its context, as happens in learned and technical works. It is only possible to reduce the area of imprecision, and this can only be attained through considerable experience of the lexical item used in contrasting and parallel contexts.

At advanced levels of learning, training in the recognition of registers may be important, and lexical contrasts will be central to this work. In the matter of style, lexical variations will combine with grammatical contrasts. At the elementary stages of language learning, however, it is the grammatical contrasts which will be of greater importance, although, of course, no real grammatical system exists without lexical items to act as its exponents.

The plan of a course will list, among other things, a number of topics, mostly expressed as a grammar of the language. The index of most textbooks will show something of this kind in operation. In most present cases there is no clear reason for the sequence of items nor are there clear priorities. Moreover, inspection of the texts will rarely show many examples of the grammatical point in question. Indeed very often the first meeting with the new grammatical pattern is by way of paradigms following a text which has made little or no use of the forms.

Such a list (expressed in formal terms, not in terms of traditional grammar) should be drawn up very carefully, ensuring an order which has a care for the greater usefulness of some patterns and for the avoidance of duplication. For these reasons, past verbal forms might well precede present verbals, a grammatical subjunctive (as in French) will come very early in the course if its omission limits the use of quite basic lexical items. The future verbal forms may be so little used as to be of doubtful interest to all but the advanced student.

Once listed, the grammatical patterns will normally suggest their own situational contexts. The past/present contrast suggests that of (present) accidents and (past) reports or flashbacks, of duty done or not done; the future/present contrast is that of plans or duty to be done; the conditional verb forms belong to the hypothetical, to uncertain plans. Within a language other contrasts exist which cause difficulties to foreign learners. The imperfect/passé composé contrast in French might be illustrated in this way.

### TEXTS AND DRILLS

Teaching point: contrast of tense/aspect imperfect/passé composé. FRENCH.

Jean Aboutiret travaillait dans les bureaux d'administration d'une vieille compagnie originaire de Lyon. Il travaillait là depuis douze ans et était l'ami de tous. Il suivait chaque jour la même routine et ne regrettait point l'absence de toute ambition. Il ressentait, au contraire, un calme et une sécurité qui allaient fort bien ensemble.

Il louait une petite maison près de la ville, il avait une femme qui vieillissait avec grâce et trois enfants qui grandissaient sagement. Il n'avait pas de voiture, ne cherchant aucune responsabilité de cette sorte. Il se rendait à l'usine tous les jours par le même autobus, arrivant exactement à la même heure chaque matin.

Un matin que l'autobus arrivait au terminus, où il descendait chaque jour, M. Aboutiret a pris son manteau et le journal qu'il achetait tous les jours pour être comme tous les autres. Il s'est levé et s'est dirigé tranquillement vers la sortie. Il était justement sur le point de descendre quand deux hommes l'ont saisi et ont parlé avec lui pendant quelques instants. Puis il les a accompagnés vers une petite camionnette où ils lui ont montré quelque chose à la dérobée. M. Aboutiret a blanchi puis s'est retourné et a marché vers l'entrée de l'usine, plus vite que d'habitude; il a failli courir.

The contrast here is intended to be between a continuum of events of greatly varying duration. In fact the variety of time relevance within any account of this kind will reduce the significance of any more specific time reference which the English learner would want to impart. In the above text it is intended to increase the

general, unbroken aspectual significance of the verbal forms compared with the chain of discrete events signalled by the 'passé
composé'. It is useful, and easy, to develop a story throughout the
various texts. Parallel texts can reinforce the contrast, maintaining
the interest by certain discrepancies of fact between them. Here is
a sample text which uses very much the same vocabulary as the
previous text. However, the formal contrast is intended to work
slightly in the opposite direction, with the emphasis on the series
of discrete events at the centre of the plot. Further texts would be
possible from, say, an eye-witness. These texts might well use the
'passé composé' throughout, since they would be concerned solely
with the sequence of events.

Je venais par le même autobus que tous les jours et je regardais, comme
toujours, les autres passagers qui entraient et sortaient: des connaissances,
des amis, et comme toujours quelques inconnus. Naturellement je
m'intéressais à tout ce monde, affairé pour rien, et les inconnus, dont
la plupart étaient des jeunes gens et des jeunes femmes qui cherchaient
du travail ou arrivaient pour commencer leur première journée de travail.
Ce matin-là, pourtant, j'ai remarqué deux hommes inconnus qui atten-
daient au coin en face du terminus.

Ces deux inconnus se sont approchés de moi et m'ont demandé la
route la plus directe vers la mairie. Je leur ai offert de la leur montrer
sur une carte, ne connaissant pas très bien le système de circulation dans
la ville. Je les ai accompagnés vers leur camionnette pour consulter leur
carte et puis j'ai dû me dépêcher pour ne pas être en retard.

The content may be slightly altered at each reporting (as is the
way in human affairs). There is already a slight discrepancy in the
two accounts given here and this could be continued. The changes
are carried by the lexis; the grammatical content remains consistent.

In drawing up the initial list, information will be taken from a
contrast of native language and foreign language patterns. These
areas of interference often present few problems for the learner.
Difficulties are more likely to come from different structuring *within*
the foreign language rather than from different structuring *between*
languages. The frequent use of reflexive verb forms in French is
less difficult than knowing which verbs prefer this form to an in-
transitive use of the non-reflexive; the *distinctions* between the
German particles present difficulties greater than those of their use.

Decisions concerning this preliminary inventory of linguistic
items will be based principally on the range of possible collocation
of the lexical items and the width of use of grammatical patterns.
Within the scope of these items completeness is less important than

thoroughness. The establishment of detailed *pedagogical grammars* rather than *linguistic grammars* lies in the future. For the moment, however, the distinction is an important one.

A linguistic grammar will state everything about a language to the best of its ability; the pedagogical grammar will state all those things about a language which are relevant to its teaching, and will state them in a way that bears on the teaching. Frequency counts of vocabulary (collocations and co-occurrence) and, in time, of grammatical structures (contextual co-occurrence and contrast) will provide some of the details for a pedagogical grammar. The learner will not, of course, meet forms from the informal register of the language even though paradigms are incomplete without the second person singular pronouns and verb forms. The passive form may well be taught only if no other patterns are available; or the passive forms will be the *only* ones taught. Whatever items are selected they must be irreplaceable and relevant to use and they must be taught 'to a purpose'.

The teacher may draw up a linguistic inventory or he may be faced with an existing, unchanging one. In either case an analysis of the internal structure of the grammatical or other points thought worthy of attention will indicate the areas where attention will be needed most. The ideas of the language are confused by distracters from the written usage. It is also probably hidden, for many language teachers, by falsely 'complete' paradigms, by simplicist 'rules' not based on use, by long lists of 'irregular' forms which are not 'regular' or 'irregular'.

If phonological/morphological analysis is made using a broad, phonemic transcription and syntactical analysis by means of a system of symbols, much that is otherwise hidden becomes plain. Here are a number of teaching points from French. These have been expressed in IPA notation; readers to whom phonetic transcription is new will nevertheless find it rewarding to make the effort to follow the changes and relationships.

PHONOLOGY

Contrastive sounds which present difficulties are

/y/u/ /ø/œ/ /ɛ/e/ /ã/ɔ̃/ /ɛ̃/œ̃/ /y/uːw/ /i/e/

These may be exemplified, respectively, by such pairs of words as: dû/doux peu/peur serais/serai langue/longue brin/brun lui/Louis dix/dé.

The difficulty of setting these phonemic contrasts in meaningful sentences without surrounding them with a mixed bag of sounds has been discussed earlier. It is possible to construct a limited number of sentences contrasted by one of the phonemic contrasts suggested above.

J'en ai peu/j'en ai peur
/ʒã ne pø/ʒã ne pœːr/

Donnez-moi des timbres/donnez-moi dix timbres
/dɔne mwa de tɛ̃br/dɔne mwa di tɛ̃br/

Such minimally contrastive pairs can be used for training in sound-discrimination and in careful production. Most of such training, however, will rely on work with single sounds or in single words since this is the only way to focus attention on the sound itself.

If time is available considerable attention may be given to training in discrimination and production of sounds. The course might first of all contrast contiguous sounds in the native and foreign languages, then go on to ask the learner to repeat only the foreign sound. For example:

Listen: day/dé, i.e. /dei/de/; day/dé; day/dé.
Now repeat the second sound in each pair:

day/dé; may/mai; lay/les; Kay/quai
/de/     /me/      /le/      /ke/

Now repeat only the French sound when you hear it. If you are right you will hear a voice repeat the sound after you:

day # / (bell or other signal) de / # de (bell, etc.) mai / # mai (bell)
Kay / # (bell)

Work of this kind might be far more extended and staged. It would be followed by work in phonemic contrasts of sounds introduced in this way. Alternatively, the sounds would be contrasted entirely in the foreign language from the start:

Listen: boue (i.e. /bu/), doux (/du/), sou, moue...
Now listen: boue/bu; doux/du; sou/su; moue/mû...
Repeat the first sound only: boue/bu; doux/du...
Now repeat that sound when you hear it: boue; du; sou; mû; doux...

When the sounds are placed in sentences, some use can be made of the phonological environment. The production of sound /y/ might be helped by being used in a sentence like this.

il moulait la scie; la scie est mouillée, où est-elle? Elle est unique.
/il mulɛ la si; la si ɛ mwije, uwɛtɛl? ɛl ɛt ynik/

The alternation of front vowel /i/ and back vowel with lip-rounding /u/ prepares the way for the front vowel with lip-rounding /y/.

Another type of phonological environment could be to set the required sound within or as an extension of the direction required for the production of other sounds. For example, /ɛ/ lies phonetically between /a/ and /y/ in 'l'argent est sur la table'. /e/ lies phonetically between /ə/ and /i/ in 'le pré brille sous le soleil'.

Work of this kind is time-consuming, and involves sounds and sentences which can be of little relevance to the learner. It is doubtful if the time can be justified when there is so much grammatical and lexical work to be done. This does not, of course, apply to the language specialist, for whom a near-native pronunciation is essential. Those learners for whom communication is the sole requirement will need more attention to items of grammar and vocabulary, which will, of course, involve the phonology of the language. The teacher must decide whether a systematic approach to pronunciation is to be adopted. Separate topics in pronunciation *may* be taken where a blockage to communication is likely to develop, but systematic pronunciation practice which attempts to cover everything, in spite of severely limited time is useless. In other words, the ten minutes spent at the beginning of each lesson on pronunciation practice is better given over to more practice of the major topics of the course.

### MORPHOLOGY

In operational terms an adjective may have one, two or three forms in French:

it may be invariable (a lexical item);
one form may collocate with plural forms (les, des or de) defined operationally /lwajo/;
one form may collocate with la or une.

Some base forms ending in a vowel also have a form (very like the form collocating with la) used before a word beginning with a vowel.

An analysis of French adjectives might work from base forms such as the following:

1. /vɛr/pti/tu/kɔ̃dɥi/favɔri/
2. /frɛ/blɑ̃/frɑ̃/
3. /ru/gro/gra/du/
4. /ekski/œrø/

5. /grã/
6. /lɔ̃/
7. /ruʒ/kɔ̃ble/fini/larʒ/riʃ/pyblik/syperjœr/
8. /vif/primitif/tardif/

When co-occurring with la or une, groups 1–6 add a consonant, /t/ʃ/s/z/d/g/ respectively. Group 7 is invariable and group 8 voices the final consonant (i.e. /f/ /v/).

An analysis of this kind will suggest a regularity which can be used for teaching and will allow a large number of adjectives to be included in the patterns which would otherwise be listed as 'irregular'.

The verbal forms in French show the following. (I have left the paradigms with their usual '6-person' format to remind the reader of the traditional approach. The paradigms could obviously be reduced on the basis of their formal exponents.)

A. /done/ ('donner')

Pattern 1 (usually 'present tense')

1. root morpheme /dɔn/    4. +/ɔ̃/
2.                        5. +/e/
3.                        6. root morpheme (i.e. +Θ)

(a sub-group /rãdr/ adds /d/ to the root morpheme /rã/ everywhere but 1, 2, 3 of pattern 1).

(/dɔrmiːr/ etc. might be regarded as a sub-group of A in pattern 1.)

B. /finiːr/

Pattern 1

1. root morpheme /fini/    4. +/sɔ̃/
2.                         5. +/se/
3.                         6. +/s/+Θ (i.e. just /s/)

(a sub-group (e.g. /liːr/ /prɔdɥiːr/) has /z/ instead of /s/).

Pattern 2 (usually 'future tense')

A (not sub-group) /əre ərɔ̃/    B (and sub-group of A) /(r)e (r)ɔ̃/
                  /əra əre/                              /(r)a (r)e/
                  /əra ərɔ̃/                              /(r)a (r)ɔ̃/

(N.B. outside the paradigm (i.e. functionally) there are just three forms /(ə)re/əra/ərɔ̃/.)

Pattern 3 ('imperfect')

has endings /ɛ/ in 1, 2, 3
            /jɔ̃, je, ɛ/ in 4, 5, 6
with the prefix /s/ or /z/ as in pattern 1.

Other patterns interrelate in an obvious way. This partial analysis, however, indicates ways in which regularity of patterning could be used more effectively if the teaching were functional and not based on a classification by conjugational and tense paradigm listing which has historical significance but no direct operational use. The use of the traditional paradigm in the above analysis is intended to show the two approaches in contrast. The paradigm is sometimes a useful shorthand for an operational (formal) definition which has more relevance to the teaching itself. Verb forms given as 1, 2, 3 and 5 collocate with singular nominals, while 4, 5 and 6 collocate with plural nominals. These terms 'singular' and 'plural' can themselves be defined operationally within the structure of the language. Verb forms given at 2 in each pattern are appropriate to a register of the language which must be defined within that language. Their use, moreover, must be decided on the grounds of situational relevance to the learner. Clearly German 'du' is less restricted than French 'tu' and clearly few learners will heed these forms for some time. If within the language the verbal forms belonging to specifically informal/formal register contrasts are exactly the same as otherwise collocated verbal forms, and consistently so, then the contrast is elsewhere and the verbal form may be used in utterances where the marker is lexical.

> 'You're crafty!'
> 'You're wise in the ways of the world'

The presentation text may introduce only verb forms 3 and 6 in a narrative, or may also include 1, 4 and 5 if in the form of a dialogue. A commentary made by the learner will almost certainly be in verb forms 3 and 6 unless he is directed to involve himself in the situation. At some time, in any case, his use of verb forms 1 and 5 will need to be increased. This can be done by presenting a number of parallel texts which will remove the restriction to one or two verb forms only. The introduction to the verb forms must be operationally based. What is needed will be used. The introduction of paradigms is a waste of time, and so is teaching which follows the (artificial) pattern of the paradigm.

Analysis of the sentence will often show morphological changes only half-perceived through the writing system. For example, one pattern of plural formation in French might be expressed phonemically as

$$\left. \begin{array}{l} /a \\ /\partial \end{array} \right\} > e/ \ \text{ and } \ /\varepsilon > s\tilde{o}/,$$

e.g. le machiniste est déjà en retard > les...sont... another as + /ez/ and /ε > sɔ̃/, e.g. /loːtr trɛ̃ ε prε/ > /lezoːtr trɛ̃ sɔ̃ prε/. These changes, rather than the incidentals of exponential shape (how they are written), will show where the patterns are to be found.

Syntactic patterns, unlike morphological ones, are best clarified by the use of a grammatical transcription. If we take /la vwatyr struːv dəvã la port/ as a matrix sentence and /ʒɔrʒ a aʃte yn vwatyr/ as the constituent sentence we want to introduce into it we may say that

$$S_{matrix} + S_{const} = N_{matrix} + /k/ + N_{const} + V_{const} + V_{matrix} + Adv,$$

(i.e. /la vwatyr k ʒɔrʒ a aʃte struv dəvã la pɔrt/). Sentences of the same structure will relate in the same way. Moreover, selection of appropriate lexical items at each point in the resultant structure will provide a carefully staged exercise in the formation of various subordinating patterns.

| | | | | | |
|---|---|---|---|---|---|
| la voiture | que Georges | a achetée | se trouve | devant la porte. |
| le cheval | que Georges | a acheté | se trouve | devant la porte. |
| le cheval | que ma femme | a acheté | se trouve | devant la porte. |
| le cheval | que ma femme | a attelé | se trouve | devant la porte. |
| le cheval | que ma femme | a attelé | mange | devant la porte. |

These analyses are already beginning to produce material which will be useful in constructing drills. Indeed there is a relationship between linguistic description and drill construction which is inescapable. This does not mean that only linguistic experts can design drills—far from it. But a linguistic 'insight', an understanding of the structure of the language, what is often called 'a feeling' for the language, is an important control over the structure of language drills. Essentially drills composed of frequent surface structure patterns are efficient; those consisting of patterns related at deep-structure level are, in the long term, more effective still.

A drill is a group of items each of which consists of a stimulus utterance or other prompt, standing in a clear relationship to a response which the learner can be expected to make. In order that the learner shall respond consistently, one pattern must be clearly in operation throughout the drill.

Most existing drills operate on behavioural principles in terms of stimulus and response. The learner hears the correct response after he has made his attempt. The correct response will indicate whether he is progressing well or not. It will also presumably act as reinforcement if, as is likely, his response is correct. The student's response will be correct if one pattern alone is being drilled, and if the linguistic relationship which is being drilled is clear from the examples given.

First: define exactly the purpose of the drill. Decide in grammatical terms what responses the learner is to make. Then decide what stimuli may call forth the response mechanically or naturalistically. A drill might be designed to practise the English simple past forms of 'weak' verbs (formed by the addition of a morpheme /d/ as against 'strong' verb formation by changing the root vowel). The drill might be like this:

> Stimulus: He looks healthy
> Response: He looked healthy (i.e. /s/ > /t/)
>   S: She cooks well
>   R: She cooked well
>   S: He works long hours
>   R: He worked long hours
>   S: They hope for more money
>   R: They hoped for more money (i.e. alternative change ⊖ > /t/)...

In this drill only verbs ending in a voiceless consonant (other than /t/) would be used. The morphophonemic pattern would be

$$\left\{ \begin{matrix} s \\ \ominus \end{matrix} \right\} > /t/$$

Another drill would deal with those verbs with a root morpheme ending in a voiced consonant (other than /d/). It will be clear that some kind of analysis of the teaching point will have been necessary before carefully programmed drills can be written. No harm is necessarily caused by mixing two linguistic features in one drill (for instance, in the example just given, if the morphophonemic relationship were already known by the learner as: voiceless consonant + /z/⊖ > voiceless consonant + /t/ voiced consonant + /s/ ⊖ > voiced consonant + /d/ /t,d + s/⊖ > /t, d + əd/), but it is important that the teacher or course designer should understand exactly what linguistic features the drill contains.

A naturalistic version of the drill just given would be:

>   S: He looks healthy
>   R: Yes, and he looked healthy last week
>   S: She cooks well
>   R: Yes, and she cooked well last week
>   S: He works long hours
>   R: Yes, and he worked long hours last week
>   S: They hope for more money
>   R: Yes, and they hoped for more money last week

The difference in this case is small, consisting solely of the addition of a lexical item. As can be seen, the difference is one of emphasis. The mechanical drill concentrates attention on one point; the naturalistic drill, while drilling precisely the same point, is dealing in useful collocational sets. Most important, the verb form is being collocated with an adverb which has a high frequency. This collocation will be important later as one 'meaning' of the simple past, i.e. for the student phonological alternations of the type

$$\left/ \quad \begin{matrix} ^{s}_{\Theta} > d, t\, d\,^{s}_{\Theta} \} > d\partial d \dots \\[2mm] t\,^{s}_{\Theta} \} > t\partial d \end{matrix} \quad \right/ \quad \dots$$

in contrast with the present perfect, i.e. for the student:

$$\text{HAVE} + \text{verbal root} + \begin{cases} \text{vowel change (including no change)} + \partial n, \\ d, t, \partial d, \end{cases} \text{etc.}$$

The principal concern of the drill is with the forms of language, leaving the presentation work to deal as far as possible with 'meaning' by context. Nevertheless, the stimulus response item can provide a certain amount of context although the bias will still be with form. The 'meaning' of the simple past is being displayed by means of a formal co-occurrence of the type:

$$\text{Past} \Rightarrow \begin{cases} (\text{simple past (as } formally \text{ defined above)} + \\ \qquad\qquad\qquad\qquad\text{last (Nom. time))} \dots \\ (\text{pres. perfect (as } formally \text{ defined above)} + \\ \qquad\qquad\qquad\qquad\text{the last (Nom. time))} \dots \end{cases}$$

Similarly in French the contrast, imperfect/passé composé, may be supported by the former's co-occurrence with depuis + numeral + Nom. time. It may be further supported by its (customary) co-occurrence with

$$\begin{matrix} \text{toutes les} + \text{Nom. time,} \\ \text{tous} \end{matrix}$$

although this may also co-occur with the passé composé. Where there is an alternation of the possibilities of co-occurrence of forms relating to one broad time-reference, in this case 'past', the option will be stylistic rather than simply grammatical. In other words, if such an alternation is possible in all instances of the particular co-occurrence, the option will be lexical and stylistic; it cannot be grammatical. The teacher may then make a choice of the form he is going to teach (much better if all language teachers could agree on which one to select) and teach it as the only one in that collocation, reserving the option until the advanced stages in which features of style may play a part.

There are a number of ways in which drills are classified, and it is unlikely that all the possible types are yet known. The forms of mechanical drill are probably all known, but the naturalistic drill can be developed further than it has been at present.

Drills are generally classified as: *repetition, incremental, substitution, conversion* (also called *mutation*) and *response*.

In phonological work drills are likely to consist entirely of repetition:

    S: Répétez: la voix
1   R: # (pause in which the student responds; 'la voix')
2   Confirmation: la voix
3   R 2 # (pause for student to respond again: 'la voix')
4   C 2: la voix (second confirmation)

Delicate work of the kind described earlier may use repetition drills to good effect. The drill shown above is *four-phase*. It allows the student two responses and lets him hear the correct response three times. There is little justification for this: in Skinnerian terms, because the student's first response will be correct; in general terms, because it uses twice as much tape, and assumes that the student will not, or cannot, rewind to hear the master cue. The drill might be three-phase:

    S:   voilà
1   R:   # (voilà)
2   C:   voilà
3   R 2: # (voilà)

The same objections apply as before.

The drill may be two-phase:

    S: la voile
1   R: #
2   C: la voile

If the student reaches the 'confirmation' only to find he has anticipated wrongly and has made the wrong response, he can rewind to the beginning of the item and do it again. This recursive technique is one which should be encouraged from the start. Such repetition drills may offer the best introduction, since few methodological complications will intervene and the student can be trained to work at an item again and again if he has any doubts about his performance.

Even when no detailed phonological training is proposed, an amount of delicate work is advisable in the introductory stage to ensure that the learner is judging his performance by sufficiently critical standards.

The drills used as examples will all be two-phase. Beware of the commercial tape with three- or four-phase drills. It may *sound* careful but the extra tape used will have added to the cost of the course.

The principal use of the *incremental drill* is to drill stress and intonational patterns. The open version may also be used to *test* knowledge of syntax:

*Fixed incremental*

    S: Répétez: Georges Meillaret
    R: ♯ Georges Meillaret
    C: Georges Meillaret. [S:] Travaillait
    R: Georges Meillaret travaillait
    C: Georges Meillaret travaillait. [S:] Jour et nuit
    R: Georges Meillaret travaillait jour et nuit...

*Open incremental*

    S: Wiederholen Sie! Ernst Neumann
    R: Ernst Neumann
    C: Ernst Neumann. [S:] Fing an
    R: Ernst Neumann fing an
    C: Ernst Neumann fing an. [S:] Der ältere
    R: Der ältere Ernst Neumann fing an
    C: Der ältere Ernst Neumann fing an. [S:] sobald
    R: Der ältere Ernst Neumann fing sobald an...

We have seen the part played by substitution in linguistic description. The *substitution drill* will obviously teach syntactic patterns and morphological relationships.

*Fixed substitution*

    S: Répétez: Je n'aime pas les repas froids
    R: Je n'aime pas les repas froids
    C: Je n'aime pas les repas froids. S: chauds
    R: Je n'aime pas les repas chauds
    C: Je n'aime pas les repas chauds. S: anglais
    R: Je n'aime pas les repas anglais
    C: Je n'aime pas les repas anglais. S: réchauffés
    R: Je n'aime pas les repas réchauffés...

*Open substitution*

S: Wiederholen Sie! Ich esse nicht gern Rindfleisch
R: Ich esse nicht gern Rindfleisch
C: Ich esse nicht gern Rindfleisch.  S: Er
R: Er isst nicht gern Rindfleisch
C: Er isst nicht gern Rindfleisch.  S: Kocht
R: Er kocht nicht gern Rindfleisch
C: Er kocht nicht gern Rindfleisch.  S: doch
R: Er kocht doch gern Rindfleisch
C: Er kocht doch gern Rindfleisch.  S: am liebsten...

In each of these pairs the open drill is really a test item, since it presupposes in both cases some syntactic awareness. Often, too, morphology alone gives no indication of the new unit's position in the sentence. The word or phrase must already be known as belonging to the same class as a unit in the existing sentence. Some control has in fact been exercised in the open drill given as an example, since there is clearly a *sequence* in the positions at which the substitution takes place. The drill might well become completely open after one such sequence, continuing as:

R: Er kocht doch am liebsten Rindfleisch
C: Er kocht doch am liebsten Rindfleisch.  S: wohl
R: Er kocht wohl am liebsten Rindfleisch
C: Er kocht wohl am liebsten Rindfleisch.  S: verkauft
R: Er verkauft wohl am liebsten Rindfleisch
C: Er verkauft wohl am liebsten Rindfleisch.  S: Zigarren...

Such completely open drills can be severe tests of a learner's ability to handle structures.

The perceptive Germanist will have noticed that the particles 'doch' and 'wohl' could have been treated differently. 'Doch' could have replaced 'nicht gern' as a unit rather than just 'nicht'; 'wohl' could have replaced 'am liebsten'. The drill works at sentence level, and the emphasis is on the total sentence. A student responding 'er kocht doch Rindfleisch' or 'er kocht doch wohl Rindfleisch' would not be as disconcerted as the student who had responded *'Doch kocht nicht gern Rindfleisch' and so on. There is a difference in the quality of these 'errors' (one real, one *ad hoc*) which is inherent in the nature of the drill and which is clear to the student in practice. In any case the student making the *ad hoc* 'error' is doing well with his German.

The *conversion drill*, often called the 'mutation drill', has affinities with the transformations with which some descriptive linguists work. The conversion drill certainly can function in a way reminiscent of the native speaker's operational procedure in patterning his language.

Although the incremental and substitution drills worked with sentences, their principal concern was with the linguistic item as a member of a class. The conversion drill deals with the relationship between whole sentences, operating through one morphological or lexical change or several. Indeed, the change, although patterning consistently throughout the drill, may be considerable between stimulus and response, as with the change from active to passive constructions.

*Fixed conversion*

    S:  Il connaît vos amis
    R:  Il ne connaît pas vos amis
    C:  Il ne connaît pas vos amis
    S:  Il voit les enfants
    R:  Il ne voit pas les enfants
    C:  Il ne voit pas les enfants...

The change is consistent, here adding /n/ to /il/ and /pa/ to the verb. If a stimulus sentence contained a verb beginning with a vowel, the change would be different, adding /n/ as a prefix to the verb, /il natãpa lotobys/ for example. Whether the drill is restricted to the one change or includes sub-group changes of this kind will depend on the learner's previous experience and whether he is accustomed to the formal change. Here /n/ functions as a suffix to the subject, or as a prefix to the main verb or auxiliary when that begins with a vowel, which is merely an aspect of French syllabification.

A constituent sentence may be combined with a matrix sentence in the way already suggested for French in this chapter. In German the drill would be as follows:

    S:  Die Wand ist frisch bemalt. Sie haben den Mantel an die Wand
        gehängt
    R:  Die Wand, woran Sie den Mantel gehängt haben, ist frisch bemalt
    S:  Der Wagen steht vor der Tür. Erich hat den Wagen neulich gekauft
    R:  Der Wagen, den Erich neulich gekauft hat, steht vor der Tür

In German the pause before the subordinate clause (marked by a comma) is non-optional. In English there is the further complication of the pause as an option before adjectival clauses (defined operationally). The option can be ignored in the conversion drill, a drill in turn dealing with patterns of the type:

(*a*) The car which Henry drove is broken
(*b*) The car, which Henry drove, is broken
(*c*) The car that Henry drove is broken (no option)

As usual, a priority must be established. Pattern (*a*) may be taught first. Pattern (*c*) need not be taught in this usage until a fairly advanced stage of learning since (*a*) is useful and can be used as one part of a meaningful option later. For the most elementary stages the pattern (*d*) 'The car Henry drove is broken' would be preferred. The option (*a*)/(*b*) can be dealt with in an echo response drill.

As well as calling for transformation to the negative or interrogative or past, etc., the conversion drill may require changes in formal pattern when it co-occurs with a certain additional unit of the language. For example:

S: Precede each utterance with 'il faut que', making all the necessary changes.
S: Jean arrive demain
R: Il faut que Jean arrive demain
C: Il faut que Jean arrive demain
S: Roger prend un taxi
R: Il faut que Roger prenne un taxi...

or

S: Precede each utterance with 'als ob', making the necessary changes.
S: Er war schon gekommen
R: Als ob er schon gekommen wäre
C: Als ob er schon gekommen wäre
S: Sie hatten ihm 20 Bücher geschenkt
R: Als ob sie ihm 20 Bücher geschenkt hätten

The principle of systematic co-occurrence within language can be extended further, introducing lexical stimuli for formal changes, in:

*Triggered conversion*

S: Repeat: He knows your friends
R: He knows your friends
C: He knows your friends
S: Last year
R: He knew your friends last year
C: He knew your friends last year
S: Two years ago
R: He knew your friends two years ago
C: He knew your friends two years ago

S: Next year
R: He'll know your friends next year
C: He'll know your friends next year...

Here the verb form changes in association with changes in the (lexical) adverbials. Such collocation is an important part of the the individual learner's mapping-out of 'meaning'.

A combination of the triggered conversion drill and the open substitution drill is possible. Such a drill has been called 'open-end mutation'

S: Répétez: Charles Guyard s'est assis devant la porte
R: Charles Guyard s'est assis devant la porte
C: Charles Guyard s'est assis devant la porte
S: Hélène
R: Hélène Guyard s'est assise devant la porte
C: Hélène Guyard s'est assise devant la porte
S: dans le marché
R: Hélène Guyard s'est assise dans le marché
C: Hélène Guyard s'est assise dans le marché
S: installer
R: Hélène Guyard s'est installée dans le marché
C: Hélène Guyard s'est installée dans le marché
S: Negative
R: Hélène Guyard ne s'est pas installée dans le marché
C: Hélène Guyard ne s'est pas installée dans le marché

The difficulty is often that of signalling the syntactical rôle of the cue item. It would have been reasonable for a student to respond, early in this drill, with 'Charles Guyard s'est assis devant Hélène' and he would have found it difficult to proceed with the other items as a result. Care has to be taken to use whatever signals may be available and a code can be established within a group which will overcome this difficulty. Here a name replaces a name. As with all 'open' drills, the 'open-end mutation' drill is essentially a test. It teaches little, because the items introduced rarely belong to the same class and the changes are therefore inconsistent. Whatever pattern exists appears so infrequently that it will not be apparent unless the learner already knows it. However, such drills do provide useful revision and reinforcement work and can be so devised as to provide really searching tests of a student's control of the structures involved.

The *response drill* is the most naturalistic. It may establish a linguistic (transformational) relationship between stimulus utterance and response, a lexical relationship, or it may deal with a contextual relationship.

*Echo response*

> S: He can play the piano
> R: He can't, can he?
> C: He can't, can he?
> S: Sue can swim
> R: She can't, can she?...

Here the relationship is a linguistic one. The relationship might simply be situational:

> S: He can play the piano
> R: You don't say so!...

The relationship might be lexical:

> S: Il y va chaque jour
> R: Oui, il y va tous les jours
> C: Oui, il y va tous les jours
> S: Il nous téléphone chaque mois
> R: Oui, il nous téléphone tous les mois...

> S: He's a lorrydriver
> R; Oh, he drives a lorry, does he?
> S: He's a hotel manager
> R: Oh, he manages a hotel, does he?...

From this point the confirmation will be omitted, although we shall return to it in considering the scripting of drills.

Very often the only difference between the response drill and a conversion drill is that the former is more concerned with the naturalness of the response. The possibility of introducing lexical items whose 'meanings' are already known and collocating them with difficult formal or lexical alternations can be very useful indeed. For example the option mentioned earlier in this chapter (page 124) in the case of English adjectival clauses may be clarified by differential collocation:

> S: The car which Henry bought is broken
> R: Oh, that one
> S: The car, which Henry bought, is broken
> R: Oh, he did, did he?

or

> R: He bought it anyway, did he?

> S: We stopped playing tennis
> R: You don't play tennis now?
> S: We stopped to play tennis
> R: You play tennis now?

S: We stopped eating pork
R: You don't eat pork now?...

S: Sie sagt, er sei krank
R: Sie weiss ja *nicht*?
S: Sie sagt, er ist krank
R: Sie weiss das bestimmt?
S: Franz sagt, die anderen seien abgefahren
R: Er weiss ja *nicht*?...

The response drill may be contextualised by picture prompts, by a narrative, by any situation known or seen. The contextualised response drill is very similar indeed to the presentation or revision text. The prompt must be carefully designed to avoid ambiguity, since the contextual control will be replacing a very close linguistic control in other drill types. Nevertheless, some prompts may be derived from the situation shared within the school or college

S: What time does the library open?
R: It opens at 4
S: What time does it shut?
R: It shuts at 5
S: On what floor is the library?
R: It's on the ground floor...

Such 'drills' are really only a substitute for well-designed presentation and revision material. They are useful reminders of material and can form a partial introduction to oral composition. Nevertheless they do not drill, since they are unlikely to present a sufficiently tight internal organisation. The patterns, if they exist, are diffuse and the content therefore tends to be related closely to clear situational or contextual prompts.

On the other hand, the 'linguistic' drill needs some contextual connexion with presentation or other texts if it is not to become so irrelevant as to become uninteresting for the student. Drills form part of the course and are then related grammatically to the presentation material. One or two items in each drill should also be related lexically. Remedial drills may be related more to the needs of certain students than to the content of the presentation material. As far as possible, however, one or two items should present harmonics with the lexical content of previous material. The other items in the drill should revise a range of vocabulary already known by the student. A few new lexical items can be introduced into a drill of formal relationships. This will emphasise to the learner that formal comprehension does not depend on lexical understanding, and will also ensure that future presentation material has some items already familiar to the learner.

| Type of error | Type of drill |
|---|---|
| morphological | substitution (conversion) |
| syntactical | conversion or substitution |
| phonological | listening and repetition |
| intonation, etc. | incremental |
| lexical | response |

This table is not intended to suggest hard-and-fast rules. Response drills will give collocational 'meaning' to forms practised in other drills. Lexical items are the most difficult items to retain in language, even for the native speaker, and are the least indispensable. The student's 'store' of lexical items is bound to be more fluid than that of grammatical structures and, indeed, remedial work need not deal with lexis to the same extent as grammar. Any large-scale fallout of vocabulary suggests that the presentation material has not completely done its job and that parallel texts would provide the necessary larger context which is absent from the drill.

Material has so far been discussed mainly in terms of purely aural-oral work. This is perhaps a necessary redressing of the recent balance. The written language has previously been dominant, with any oral work probably starting from the written word. We are now able to work in the spoken language and to relate the written word to it, rather than the other way round.

Our first concern is with the spoken language in its lexis, its grammar and its phonology In English we shall teach 'It isn't' and 'aren't I?', in French '/vzave/' and '/sɛpa/', in German the particles, from an early stage Material constructed on these principles is presented aurally.

In preparations for recording, in programming and scripting, and in recording itself, standards must be high. Whatever is recorded must be accompanied by a script. Unlike the written word, the recorded word is hidden from easy reference and the script alone will permit a quick check on all the contents of a tape.

The first draft of drills or text will be followed by a recording script. This should bear the name of the writer, or writers, of the material and the date of recording. It should next state: language, teaching point. It should bear a tape index number and should state the tape counter figures for the beginning and end of the material.

H. H. Smith            January 196–
     FRENCH: VERB FORMS      Tape F 2 0000–0123

Against each drill should be stated briefly type and teaching point.

Present > aller + infin. Fixed Conversion

Example, listen:

    S: il arrive.  R: il va arriver
    C: il va arriver
    S: elle danse.  R: elle va danser
    C: elle va danser

Now do the same:

    S: il arrive
    #
    C: il va arriver
    S: elle danse
    #
    C: elle va danser
    S: nous soupons
    #
    C: Nous allons souper...

All this information is recorded. In the example, the student hears the stimulus followed by a recorded response showing him what he is expected to do. This is followed immediately by the confirmation. In the main body of the drill the stimulus is followed by a pause (marked #). The pause lasts twice the length of time it would take a native speaker to make the response. The pause is followed immediately by the confirmation. After that comes the next stimulus.

No instructions are given. The pattern should be clear in the example (in the light of students' knowledge of that point)—if not, the material needs to be rewritten. It will be seen that the example and the first two items of the body of the drill are identical. There is something of a tradition that each drill should consist of eight items (some say ten). In truth the optimum number of good drill items is non-finite. It is easier to select from an abundance than from a sufficiency.

Recording standards should be as high as possible. If accommodation is available egg boxes will provide a very decorative sound-proofing material. A tape-recorder in the £60 range will normally have the necessary characteristics for good recording and £10 will purchase a good (if not outstanding) microphone. Care should be taken to see that the tape transport on the recorder is quiet.

The atmosphere during recording should be relaxed; mistakes are more likely to be made when the atmosphere is tense. There should be a script for each person taking part, and the script should be clear and straightforward, with lots of 'white space'. Once the recording volume and the tape counter have been set, the recording can proceed.

When the recording has been completed the box should be clearly marked to show its status as a master or console tape, a note of its contents, and the associated script should be filed safely.

To keep silence during pauses while maintaining the necessary good pace and quality of performance in the rest of the material is extremely tiring. There are devices which will expand pauses when a tape is being copied. When these are fully developed it will be possible to record material straight through, making a fractionally longer hesitation where a pause is needed. The tape can then be copied and the significant hesitations will be expanded to any number of times their length. Meanwhile such variation of pauses and fluency must be part of the language teacher's expertise.

The introduction to language, it has been suggested, will be by way of the spoken word. The course material may be designed in terms of phonic substance or graphic substance alone. Where the course is free of external pressures other than that of relevance to certain functional requirements, careful consideration should be given to the amount of each of the four main skills to be included and even more attention should be given to the balance of spoken and written language. The strength of tradition will emphasise the part to be played by the latter, whereas a functional description of the terminal behaviour will emphasise the former. Where both are required the introduction of the written forms will be delayed, it has been suggested, until the student feels himself competent in dealing with the spoken language without need of the written language in justification.

The delay may also be extended when it is anticipated that the written language will interfere with pronunciation. There is some disagreement about the order in which reading and writing should be introduced. In his book *Language and Language Learning* (1959), Nelson Brooks summed up his views on this question: 'He (the learner) should read only what he has spoken. He should write only what he has read.' This runs counter to the close relationship between stimulus and response which is one of the characteristics of the new techniques. The relationship between words seen and words spoken or heard is close, but words seen and spoken or heard in large contexts are related far more vaguely. Words written and words spoken may have a closer, even patterned, relationship within the short utterance. Moreover, the introduction of graphic substance must call for participation by the student of a more active kind than simply reading.

In Chinese there can be little relationship learnt between phonic and graphic substance. The spoken language and the written language must be learnt separately. In other languages writing may be introduced at syllable or word level. In some European languages, notably Russian, Spanish and Italian, the written language can be taught in a very regular pattern of relationship of letter to sound. Some complication exists in Russian for English learners as a result of certain graphic variations from Roman letters, and by a stress which changes the value of vowels in the word or phrase unit. The degree of regularity in both these events, however, makes the learning of both a comparatively small matter. In the case of those languages where some regularity exists between pronunciation and the written forms the relationship is, of course, only in this direction. It is possible to write from dictation but never possible to pronounce from such notation. Moreover, the regularity exists only when the matter is dictated as separate words with no concern for the phonological environment which would lead to allophonic variation in normal pronunciation of the language.

Even in languages where there is a wide and varying divergence between phonic and graphic substance at all levels, some regularity exists. In English 'heat', 'meat', 'seat', 'peat' show a regular phonic-graphic relationship. So, of course, do 'lead' and 'read' until the former functions as a nominal and the latter as a past verbal form. As the poem says:

> Beware of heard, a dreadful word
> That looks like beard and sounds like bird

In French, patterns do exist (midi, parti, sorti, rougi) but not very extensively, especially when there are morphemes recognised only in writing: 'il est parti' would otherwise pattern well with 'elle est partie' (once the spelling of /ɛl/ had been learnt). In languages of this kind a lot of rote learning must take place, aided by those regularities which can be pointed out in practice, and by frequent acquaintance with written texts.

The very first introduction should be to writing, and the writing of language already being spoken. Reading should follow very soon, again material already spoken or understood aurally. Dictation should be given in short utterances, not in words, and this should be so at all levels of proficiency. The sound-symbol relationships will be used in their normal group forms and, at the same time, dictation practice of a useful kind will be given. Words may be dictated, but this is similar to phonological training with single words. It may be useful, but it is hardly efficient. In general, dictation should deal in groups from the first:

*Jean est parti/ *à midi/. Il a *pris le *train de *trois *heures
/ʒɑ̃ɛparti/  amidi/  ilapriltrɛ̃dtrwazœːr/

The words marked with an asterisk in the above would need to be learnt separately in their written form.

Reading of texts related to language already known would be introduced as material for extensive reading. Questions are concerned with information at paragraph and higher levels. The student is encouraged to read as much as possible. Occasionally there are intensive reading assignments, when questions are concerned with details at sentence level. Gradually students' extensive reading can follow the direction of individual interests. Discussion, essays and some class sessions will show how well this reading is progressing.

At advanced stages of proficiency in the general course the emphasis will change to the written language. However, the learner's specialist requirements may include acquaintance with particular registers of the spoken or written language. The provision of specialised listening material will call for individual listening equipment.

At the advanced stages of the general course the learner will need a very deep understanding of the daily life (and its associations) of the foreign community. Both reading material and listening material will aim at this.

A full-scale general course would feature the following:

1. aural recognition of common grammatical patterns and all the common alternations;

2. familiarity with social aspects of the life of the speech-community and sufficient understanding of all aspects of that life for comprehension of press and radio references to events by way of harmonics of meaning (e.g. 'big and little Neddy' in Britain; 'the primaries' in U.S.).

3. phonemic, allophonic and intonational discrimination, including both semantic differences and functional differences (the association of phonological features with styles of language, e.g. /eːm ɔːfņ ða/ contrasting with /aim ɔfņ ðɛə/ 'I'm often there');

4. the extension of vocabulary by means of affixal morphemes, etc. (e.g. recognise-recognition);

5. reading (intensive and extensive) and writing skills of the same level of proficiency as in the native language (possibly even better), including the stylistic production of the written language.

## 8. EQUIPMENT

> While no efficient teaching of language first and letters second is possible without them, the concentration on the inanimate and external components of foreign language instruction has diverted attention from its more fundamental components: time, the rôle of the teacher, the nature of the foreign language learning process, the structure of the teaching environment, and —oh yes—the student.
>
> ALBERT VALDMAN, *Modern Language Journal* (May 1964)

We are undoubtedly on the verge of something like a revolution in material, equipment and, most important of all, in the attitude of teachers to handing over some of their present activities. Many of the present functions of the language classroom: the presentation of texts, drill rehearsal, sound-discrimination and pronunciation practice, and even much of the extension by parallel texts and re-combination, will be the rôle of the machine. The teacher will be freed for the critical tasks of organising the display sessions, preparing course material, producing supplementary material, adding to and improving the efficiency of the batteries of tests.

Many teachers are worried that machines will put them out of work. On the contrary, machines will release them from monotony, doing many jobs more efficiently, allowing them to give their time and effort to the planning and educative aspects of language teaching.

For the new teacher the most immediate problem in the normal classroom situation is the fluidity of the class, even the room that may seem to change shape and contents for no reason at all. Human beings are, after all, very mobile things. No teacher, however good, can expect no interruption, no change in group dynamic, no change in the atmosphere because the holiday's come or the painters are in. The problem with adults is less acute. Even here, however, group dynamic may vary considerably, and there are domestic and business worries which will intrude just as much as the painters!

The teacher has traditionally attempted to bring stability by stern discipline or by pinning pictures everywhere. The blackboard has usually been the most stable item in the classroom.

Within the limits of his ability at drawing, the teacher has been able to use the blackboard to focus attention and to impress a class with the impact of a situation or the shape of a paradigm. The blackboard, for all its constancy, has, of course, always been a difficult demonstrator of reality. The image on the blackboard has usually been a fixed one (fixed indelibly by the words 'PLEASE LEAVE' attached to a minor work of art).

This limitation in the blackboard's 'mobility' has been of little importance in the past, since the traditional language course has, above all, ascribed to language a 'rigor mortis'. Its limitation becomes more important when the new approach to language teaching is emphasising the mobility and fluidity of language in practice.

The felt cloth or flannelgraph introduces a little more 'mobility' but is more suited to revision and recombination work than to presentation and transfer. The slower progression necessary with young children makes the slow construction of situations, which the flannelgraph offers, of particular value in the primary school. Older children and adults require a more dynamic presentation and a closer approach to clarity of situation.

The illustration of most language-teaching points depends on consistency of presentation. Whereas the written language is linear, the spoken language calls for the handling of a number of variables simultaneously. The teacher unaided will almost certainly be incapable of the high standard of consistency of production of phonology, syntax, morphology and lexis on which learning of the spoken language will depend. Even the trained native speaker finds it impossible to keep the large number of variables constant throughout frequent repetition. Fatigue apart, the teacher must also listen attentively to the students' performance, and maintain a group dynamic amongst what is essentially an amorphous group of human beings.

The presentation of context adds further problems. The student has a right to demand that presentation material be relevant and interesting. Although linguistic content and contextual content are closely related, the student's concern will be with the latter. In considering motivation I have already dealt with the importance of relevance and interest.

Clearly the nature of visual material will depend on the perceptual ability of the students. 'Gestalt' psychology would suggest that perception must be applied to a total field and that it must envisage a total goal. The language-learning situation requires a control over the visual material to ensure an immediate link between the target language and context presented. A situation needs to be presented first in the smallest viable units for communication; let us call these units 'utterances' to distinguish them from the morpheme of formal linguistic analysis.

The link suggests then that the visual unit must be related to the utterance in sound. The unit of visual material will need to be as clear as possible. It will be presented several times and will be just one of a number of units so presented. These units, moreover, must be seen by the learner to be contributing to a total situation, which must be attained as soon as each of the contributing units (or, rather, its associated 'utterance') is under the learner's control. The presentation device must enable the unit of visual material to be shown repeatedly and to be shown to be adding up to a larger whole.

The illustrated textbook, like the wall picture and the blackboard, is too static to deal with the needs of dynamic language teaching. The teacher cannot be expected to produce material *ad hoc* and to present it efficiently—or even reliably—while carrying out the other activities mentioned earlier in this chapter.

There is another advantage, not yet generally realised, which results from handing over the presentation work to equipment. When the teacher must carry the burden of presenting the material, he is fully associated with the stages, many artificial, on the way to control of the target language. By some process of imprinting he comes to be associated with the means rather than the end. A truism often overlooked by the teacher is that any stage less than control of the language is less than language, and linguistic items less than grammatical constructs are so much gibberish. Much of the grammar and pronunciation drill-time is for the student practice in less than language. The teacher is easily associated with these not-quite-language sessions, and can find it hard to return the class to real communication. If, on the other hand, the visual and aural material and equipment take over this mechanical non-language or part-language work, the teacher can fade out these teaching aids and face the class with a situation in which they will not expect him to go into a sub-routine of non-language.

Teachers have rarely specified what they have been seeking as equipment; probably they have seldom been clear about it in their own minds. The factors of perception, motivation, the teaching situation and the nature of language will suggest considerations or criteria for the design and selection of language teaching equipment.

Visual equipment must enable the teacher to present the visual units (frames), each with just the amount of content he needs and no more, in such a way that a total situation can be gradually built up. This will call for equipment that can handle a large number of frames, with varying speeds of presentation and a very fast rewind. Then both the definition and the brilliance of the picture must cancel out the student's environment. Early visual equipment presented such a faint image that it could be used only in a blacked-out room. The development of bulbs and lens systems giving better definition, and the introduction of the iodine quartz lamp, make the blacking out or darkening of the room unnecessary. There is, nevertheless, an advantage in making the contrast of 'learning' environment and workaday environment considerable at some stages in the course.

Three main pieces of visual equipment are at present available: the slide/filmstrip projector; the film projector and the overhead projector. The older, stand-up type of slide projector doubles as a filmstrip projector if an attachment is available for the purpose. The newest, horizontal type of slide projector usually offers a more efficient lens system but does not allow the fitting of a filmstrip. It will, however, usually hold a greater number of slides (Plates 4 and 5).

In many ways slides are preferable to the filmstrip. It is easier to produce visual sequences with separate slides; the production of a filmstrip, unless subject to a large amount of processing afterwards, calls for very detailed planning of shots, and one mistake can easily spoil the whole production. Slides, too, may be re-sequenced, whereas the filmstrip presents an unchangeable order of events. Slides can be discarded, replaced or supplemented; the filmstrip cannot. On the other hand the interval between frames on a filmstrip is shorter than that offered between slides on any projector available. Indeed, the transition from single image to total sequenced situation is always smoother and more final with a filmstrip than would be possible with slides. Moreover, few slide projectors will hold as many images as is possible with the filmstrip.

A word here about the cineloop projector. It is cassette-loaded and uses 8 mm prepared film. With the addition of facilities for 'holding' frames and rewinding quickly, there will clearly be an increasing use of this equipment, limited only by the availability of suitable film-loops (Plate 6).

The overhead projector is a comparative newcomer to the educational scene. The light source is not very powerful, so there is no problem of noise from a cooling system, but it presents a very bright projected image. The teacher faces the class and draws or uncovers an image which is projected. This position, facing the class, is sometimes useful, but, as I have already pointed out, it is necessary for the teacher to recede from prominence in much of the classroom activity.

The need to draw images calls on an ability which the teacher may not possess, although he or she can prepare the drawings at leisure. If not, the teacher must rely on available transparencies, and there are few suitable for language teaching as yet. Alternatively, it is possible to reproduce illustrations in a form suitable for overhead projection, although the cost of this processing is at present prohibitively high.

The undoubted methodological advantage is that a visual whole can be developed stage by stage, with no break between images, as interleaved transparencies are revealed to the lens and light source. The smooth, organic development of a situation can be presented with realism. Repeated presentation from the visual unit up to the situational whole is more difficult than with the slide or filmstrip (Plates 7 and 8).

The slide/filmstrip projector should provide a sufficiently bright image without the need for a high-powered bulb. The brightness is, of course, considered in relation to the distance between projector and screen required in the teaching situation. The shortest distance is available with back-projection, and this requires a wide-angle lens on the projector. Back-projection means that the teacher must be in front of the class and this is not always an advantage. It is possible, of course, to fit the projector with remote control, and this gives the teacher some freedom of movement, although it also reduces the maximum projection speed. A tape-recorder also has to be operated. It is possible to provide a synchronising pulse on the tape which operates the slide or frame-changing mechanism in the projector. Remote control of the tape-recorder then gives control over both pieces of equipment. It is unlikely that rewinding can be accurately remote-controlled and it is, in any case, probable that the projector and playback machine will occasionally get out of phase. These considerations will limit the teacher's freedom of movement. The methodology of audio-visual and audio-lingual teaching, as described in an earlier chapter, relies on a more flexible use of equipment than is possible with remote control. It is advisable to plan the location of projector and playback equipment on the basis of the need for the equipment and the teacher to become frequently unobtrusive.

A slide/filmstrip projector should be adaptable for full frame (24 × 36 mm) or half-frame (24 × 18 mm). Most language teaching visual material uses half-frame pictures, but there are exceptions. There is also variation between filmstrips to be shown horizontally and those for vertical projection. The normal filmstrip attachment for use on a stand-up slide projector allows for both variables.

The design of equipment should make it easy to change the bulb and to fit and remove filmstrip and frame size adaptors. The slide-changing mechanism must be kind to slides and the fitting of a filmstrip must be easy (the rollers being easy to turn and the teeth of the drive rollers being kind to the holes in the filmstrip). Film-strips must always be fitted with leaders, and teachers using them must always leave them rolled ready for use, for it is hurried fitting of a filmstrip which leads to the greatest damage.

Whenever a strong light source is required, there comes the problem of cooling. If a projector is fan-cooled there will certainly be some noise. Some projectors, indeed, are *very* noisy, again a reminder of the fact that none was developed specifically for language teaching. However, it is now possible to have a projector with a bright image making noiseless convection cooling sufficient.

Noise is a problem with film projectors. Automatic film lacing is available on a number of models. It looks as though 8 mm film will become standard for educational purposes. Some work has been done, particularly in the United States, on class-composition of soundtracks in the foreign language to accompany films. This kind of work is best done by connecting film projector and tape-recorder to a synchronising unit and then recording the new soundtrack on tape. It may sometimes be advantageous if a film projector can be set to show single frames.

It will no doubt be apparent that I see little point at the moment in using film for language teaching at anything less than a very advanced level. Films that are in commercial circulation are likely to be conscious stylistic products or highly topical and therefore ephemeral. Films available for educational use are often of such poor visual and sound quality as to be highly unsatisfactory for language teaching. Films produced for language teaching are seldom of a high quality and rarely interesting. What is available scarcely justifies the purchase of a film projector.

In the matter of language-teaching films we must learn to walk before we run. I have no doubt that good language-teaching films will come from the large-scale development of good slide and film-strip material, and when videotape recorders are in wider use.

Portability is an important consideration for all equipment. Movement will shorten considerably the life of bulbs. It is preferable to reduce the movement of visual equipment and to timetable round visually equipped rooms.

Such rooms might also be equipped with tape-recorders, for, although it is less obvious, damage is again possible in movement. The quality of the tape-recorder for language teaching needs to be higher than that of the visual equipment, for accuracy of sound is clearly more important than accuracy of image, and damage to the audio-equipment is that much more serious.

The relationship between tape-recorder and language laboratory is technically so close that it is difficult to avoid duplicating many remarks about both pieces of equipment. I shall therefore consider the tape-recorder first as classroom equipment. Other technical and functional questions I shall leave until the language laboratory assembly is considered.

The classroom tape-recorder must be easy to prepare for use: the tape channel should be clear and the lacing to the take-up spool should be easy. Wind and rewind need to be fast. It is necessary to return repeatedly to the beginning of the material unless the tape has been prepared with several versions of the taped text to avoid the necessity for frequent rewinding. At the same time the brakes must be efficient but gentle enough to avoid breaking the tape. The rewind speed must be consistent no matter how small a distance the tape is rewound, and the tape-counter must be accurate, since the teacher will need frequently to rewind the space of just one utterance. The controls should be 'one-handed' and in one line so that the machine can be operated unseen if necessary (Plate 9).

The pause button assumes an unusual importance in the language classroom. It may have to be operated for fairly lengthy periods so it must be robust as well as efficient. The amplifier must be capable of reproducing accurately a wide range of sound. Since the machine will be used for recording, the microphone needs to be of high quality or, since microphones supplied with tape-recorders are rarely of high quality, the machine must be compatible with a high-quality microphone, which can be purchased separately. The tape transport must be noiseless, or recordings will feature unnecessary background hum.

No machine of the tape-recorder's delicacy and complexity can function well for long if it is cleaned and demagnetised infrequently or fed with poor-quality tape. The manual accompanying a tape-recorder will make these points—and it should be remembered that the language-teaching tape machine will be used far more frequently and roughly than will the domestic tape-recorder.

I have made little mention of the language laboratory and that has been intentional. The absence of a satisfactory name for the collection of linguistic and pedagogical principles which have developed has left a vacuum too often filled by the name of the glossiest piece of equipment to have arrived in education for a long time. The language laboratory is just a teaching *aid*, no better and no worse than the material used with it and the methods governing its use. It is not in itself a method, and there is nothing that it can do that a teacher could not do, albeit less consistently and less intensively.

The language laboratory is in origin and in essence a grouping of tape-recorders (alternatively, although not strictly a language laboratory, the grouping of students closely around one tape-recorder). It is, therefore, primarily a device for presenting the sounds of language and giving a student, alone or sharing with others, the opportunity of recording his own performance in the language and, theoretically, comparing it with the original (master) recording.

The arrangement of students sharing access to the output and input of one tape-recorder is less common and less complex than

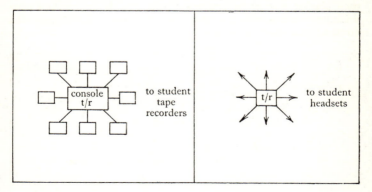

Fig. 13. Direct language laboratory arrangement.

Fig. 14. Direct language laboratory arrangement.

the grouping of tape-recorders or access to a number of tape-recorders. It is comparatively cheap; it does provide each of a small group of students with the opportunity of giving all his or her attention to the sounds of the spoken language through a headset, and permits whatever benefit there is in a comparatively untrained student listening to his or her own performance. There are signs that various developments of this 'milking machine' type of laboratory may be about to appear on the scene after some years of unpopularity.

The group of tape-recorders in the language laboratory proper are linked to a console, which is a teacher's control panel. The console will also contain a tape-recorder, possibly a record player and sometimes a radio jack. These items can be used as the sources of sound which can be recorded on to each of the student recorders. In practice input possibilities at the console, other than the tape-recorder, are seldom used. Radio programmes and records are usually taped first. Recordings are rarely satisfactory when made direct on to the student recorders through the microphone at the console. It is more practical for recordings to be made at leisure, edited as necessary, and then played on the machine at the console, the material being recorded on to the student machines.

The basic arrangement of student positions and recorders may be varied by locating each student's recorder in a centralised bank and allowing each student remote access to one machine. He may, alternatively, be given access to any one of a number of machines each playing a short programme of material. If he selects a programme from this *multi-programme bank* the material can be recorded on to a machine at his position.

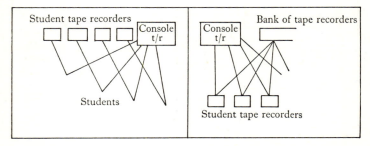

Fig. 15. Direct language laboratory arrangement.

Fig. 16. Language laboratory arrangement.

The function of the console becomes simpler in these more sophisticated arrangements; and in a highly complex arrangement, such as the distribution of programmes to a number of separate institutions, using fully self-instructional material, it may well cease to have any regular function.

At the moment the console is used for monitoring and the latter activity is essentially the act of composing on the spot new teaching material to make up for the inevitable deficiencies in existing materials. Against each booth-number on the panels of the console is a switch (sometimes two). In one position the switch makes a one-way connexion with the booth in question, allowing the teacher at the console to listen in to the student at work. There should be no signal to the student that anyone is listening, so the one-way connexion should produce no drop in volume at his machine. It seems impossible none the less to prevent some students developing a sixth sense which tells them when they are being monitored! (Plates 10 and 11).

The switch in another position gives a two-way connexion with the student booth. In some language laboratories the student's machine immediately stops, in others the student has to be invited to stop his machine, and in others the teacher may stop the student machine or not, as he wishes. In the two latter cases the teacher may make a recording on the student machine if it is still operating.

Given that work is well-programmed or the class has been carefully prepared; given that the students are known, monitoring can be speedy. One second is usually sufficient for each student; the teacher is soon able to detect whether an error has recently been made or is about to be made. It is useful if the teacher knows, at the console, if he is listening to the student at work or to a previous recording that the student himself is listening to. This can be signalled by lights at the console.

In contacting a student because an error is imminent or recent it is often possible and advisable to merge into the taped material. For this reason it is best if the student machine stops (as long as the stop is not too abrupt) or if the teacher can stop the machine. For instance, the teacher hears, as part of a drill:

(Tape) La foire a fini hier
(Student) La foire finira demain
(Tape) Le gérant est parti hier
(Student) Le gérant *partiront demain
(Teacher, stopping student machine) La foire a fini hier
(Student) La foire finira demain

(Teacher) Le gérant...
(Student) Le gérant finira demain
(Teacher) Le gérant est parti hier
(Student) Le gérant partira demain

Work on patterns is not aided by formal noises of encouragement or amazement. The student merely needs to be led back to the pattern. In no case does he deserve to be harassed by noises from his native language! Far too many teachers using language laboratories judge the quality of monitoring by the frequency of the teacher's intervention. Intervention should in fact be rarely necessary if the material is well designed and the class well prepared. Rather, the teacher should be noting any errors and planning the supplementary remedial work which will take care of them.

The laboratory may be used for what is essentially class work, where all the students are working on material within the same tape or the same part of tape, or as a library. In the latter arrangement a student takes a tape from the shelves and works at his own speed for as long as he can before lack of concentration begins. In the more complex installations he may, of course, dial for a programme from the bank of tape players, sitting either within the language laboratory or at a distant point.

It is clearly not economical to hold a set of tapes (say 20 +) for each of 15–20 classes using the facilities in any week, particularly since the class is not likely to use much more than a quarter of the taped material at any one session. The usual practice will be to transfer material from the tape-recorder at the console to the student machines. Considerable time is saved when the student machines can be set to 'record' from the console; otherwise each has to be set by hand before material can be transferred ('dubbed'). Each class can reasonably be expected to co-operate by rewinding tapes to the start at the end of each session. They could also be asked to set the machines to record, but experience suggests a high degree of unreliability in this particular matter!

On the most sophisticated installations all student machines can be fully controlled from the console. Rewinding student tapes from the console depends on an automatic stop arrangement on each student machine if a number of tapes are not to come unlaced at each rewind. This stop may be mechanically or electronically operated. Student machines equipped in this way cannot be used for private study, since tapes already on the machine cannot easily be replaced by a student with another tape. If, however, the stop devices are disconnected (or if they are not fitted) any student machines not in use may be used for private study, the student taking a tape from a small number on the shelves.

The student will fit his own tape or will (usually) sit while the material is transferred. There is little harm in this latter activity if he can record at the same time or hear his voice as he responds to the material coming from the console.

If he is there to listen to a text he will merely press the playback (or listen) button. If material has been transferred to his machine he will probably need to precede this by rewinding his tape to the beginning. If he is working at material which requires an oral response he will press the 'record' button and set the tape moving. He will record a few responses, stop the machine, rewind, stop the machine, playback. He will then either press the 'record' button or, if he is not satisfied with his performance, will rewind, stop the machine, playback. There are a number of controls to be operated each time. Since it is essential that the student on drill work should be encouraged to work as intensively as possible, a few items at a time, again and again, the controls must be simple, robust but easy to operate (Plates 12 and 13).

If he has to fit his own tape, the channelling and lacing should be easy. This can be eased by the use of cassettes of tape. These are plastic cases containing tape and two reels. The case can be slipped easily into place on the machine. They do, however, increase tape costs.

The student needs to be comfortable, since he will be concentrating for a considerable time. He will almost certainly change his sitting position frequently and this gives an advantage to the boom microphone (fixed to the headset) over the stem (or 'swan-neck') microphone, which, fixed to the student desk, will not always be in the best position for picking up the student's responses.

There is growing discussion on the value of individual student recording. For long it was assumed that recording was an integral part of the new techniques. It is indicated by a small amount of investigation that previous training in sound discrimination is essential if harm is not to be done to the student when he regularly compares his own performance with the original. Inevitably the individual's critical standards are lowered, because most people do not usually listen very carefully and are not trained phoneticians. *Long-delay feedback* (when the student compares his performance over several minutes with the original) is more harmful than *short-delay feedback* (when he is comparing item by item, recording in between). Immediate feedback is the most useful, the kind used in very delicate pronunciation training, and is available when the student's headset is *audio-active*. Such a headset, which is fairly standard with language laboratories now, will amplify the student's voice and send it to him through the earphones.

It may seem that one hears one's voice anyway whenever one speaks. The sound one hears, however, is bone-conducted and is quite different from the sound others hear—*side-tone*. If the student is to have an accurate indication of his performance as heard by others, an audio-active headset is essential.

The question of delayed feedback and its possibly unhelpful effects raises the whole question of individual recording. Comparatively few students will receive much training in assessing pronunciation, because of shortage of time, yet there will always be students who have this training or a natural ability, and for them the individual recording facility is valuable. There is also a useful aid to learning for the student in making a positive 'contribution' to the learning. It is probably best to discourage the average student from listening too much to his performance.

Most language laboratories at present available, then, are of the *listen-respond-compare* type. Of prime importance is the quality of sound reproduction, and this has not always been good enough for language work. A frequency response range of 100–8500 cycles per second is essential—with no greater variation in intensity at any point than three decibels above or below the intensity at a reference point (say 1000 c.p.s.) within the range. Most manufacturers can give a figure correct to the maximum variation in intensity—and there are test tapes. Few manufacturers, however, have reliable figures for air-to-air frequency response. However good the quality of sound at the recording and playback heads, it counts for nothing when the microphone or earphones are of poor quality. Many language laboratory manufacturers, encouraged by the apathy of purchasing authorities, still treat microphones and earphones as supplementary items. For language-laboratory work the only useful sound quality is that from microphone to recording head, from playback head to earphones.

Reproduction quality is also affected by distortion. On this, as on all technical aspects, competent independent advice should be obtained. Maintenance and the quality of tape used will in their turn affect sound-reproduction quality. It is well to remember that figures quoted by a manufacturer will be about a machine in gleaming mint condition; they are unlikely to be true after even six months of frequent use. For this reason a range of 100–10,000 c.p.s. (= 3 db) is probably a good starting-point for consideration.

Frequency response is affected considerably by the speed at which the tape is played. On most language laboratory equipment a fairly satisfactory reproduction quality is available when a tape is played at 7·5 inches per second (19 cm per second). There is often a considerable drop in quality when the speed is halved to 9·5 cm per second (3·75 i.p.s.). There are, of course, some language-laboratory activities, such as aural comprehension, advanced dictation, where a high standard of sound reproduction is not essential and the saving in tape costs which results from the slower speed is considerable. For many activities, however, any piece of equipment with less than the highest standard of reproduction available is little better than useless. The student machine should, therefore, be able to play tapes at 3·75 i.p.s., and at 7·5 i.p.s. where this is the only speed at which the full frequency range is available. Better still, all the equipment in a language laboratory installation should be capable of the full reproduction range at 3·75 i.p.s.

Both the student and the teacher need controls positioned to give the greatest ease of operation and yet allowing maximum room for reading and writing. The student needs to be able to work without undue interruption from any other student's work. It is possible, with egg-boxes or acoustic tiles, to soundproof the student booth thoroughly and the student then works in a cell. For most of the work, however, a certain amount of extraneous noise is not only harmless but probably psychologically beneficial, since the language laboratory must not be considered a place apart, divorced from the activities of the display session and real-life use of the language.

It should rarely be necessary for the student to seek the teacher's help with material. However, there may be occasional technical difficulties which will accumulate if not dealt with fairly soon after their occurrence. It is useful for the student to be able to call the teacher when he meets the rare problem. He should be able to buzz the teacher, a light remaining on against his booth number until the teacher is free to answer it. Where material is self-instructional, the call will be to a technician. It is of marginal consideration, perhaps, but both a light which does not stay on and a buzzer which keeps buzzing, can be very irritating in the intensity of language-laboratory work.

The language laboratory is likely to arouse fairly strong feelings for a number of reasons. If run well, and providing well-designed material, it will be in great demand. Its popularity will diminish if machines are often out of action. For this reason the after-sales service offered by a manufacturer should be investigated for speed and reliability. The manufacturer should be prepared to supply one or two replacement machines with the first delivery. There is an advantage in modular design, since smaller units can then be replaced easily.

It is very common for the purchase of a language laboratory to be considered as ending with the delivery and wiring of the equipment, and the construction of the booths. There are already legends about establishments which expected the new language laboratory to burst into activity and start teaching 'languages'. Those days are over, one hopes, but few purchasers consider:

*Maintenance equipment:* cleaning fluid, oil, disinfectant.

*Tapes:* student tapes normally stand up to two terms of constant use, library tapes will, of course, last longer; each taped course purchased will need to be copied if the original tapes are to be kept as 'master' tapes, away from the risk of damage; the arrival of the language laboratory may well increase the interest of teachers in preparing their own tapes of material.

*Technical care:* technical faults are cumulative, speedy correction is important. Technical supervision must be formal, with a part-time or full-time competent technician or a competent member of staff given time *each day* which is inviolate and available only for care of the laboratory.

*Spare parts:* the manufacturer's guarantee should cover *everything* unconditionally but will only last a year. After that time a recurrent grant (say $2\frac{1}{2}$–5 per cent of the original cost) must be available for the purchase of spare parts. The grant will necessarily be larger if no technician is available to carry out the repairs.

There are many reasons why the purchase of tapes, spare parts and technical supervision should be the responsibility of a regional or local school authority. The school is not a viable economic unit for these purposes and considerable savings would be possible if colleges, too, were included in a local school authority's scheme for these aspects of educational technology.

The position of the language laboratory reflects (or is reflected by) the status of its director. Administrative control will be part of the responsibilities of the head of languages where the laboratory is a respected and integral part of language work. The head of department may well need to delegate these responsibilities, but it is im-

1  Branching teaching machine (ITM).

2   Linear teaching machine (ITM).

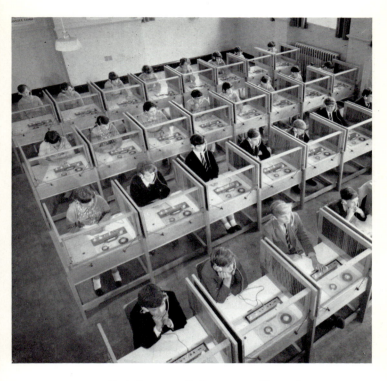

3   Rank Language Laboratory at Abersychan
    Grammar School, Mon.

4   Rank Aldis Tutor 1000 slide and filmstrip
    projector fitted with filmstrip carrier.

5  Kodak Carousel S projector.

6   Technicolor Cineloop projector.

7   3M Overhead projector in use.

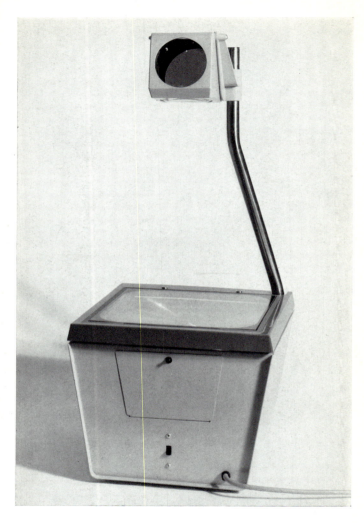

8   Close-up of 3M Overhead projector.

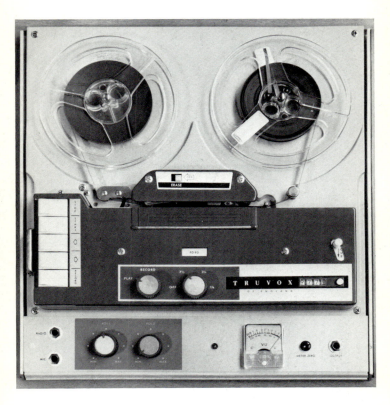

9   Truvox tape-recorder.

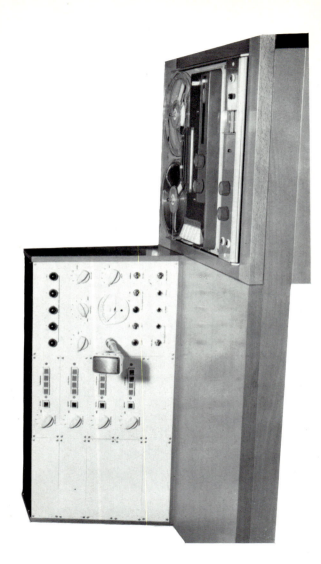

10 Console—Rank.

11  Console—Shipton.

12 Shipton student booth.

13   Rank student tape deck.

14  Audio-visual instructional device developed by Professor Carroll of Harvard.

15  The Bell and Howell Language Master can be used to bring together the pronunciation of a sentence and its written form.

16a The Opelem 'Mini-Lab' is a two-track tape-recorder on which the student records on the bottom track only. He can thus work on a duplicate master tape without any danger of erasing the original recording.

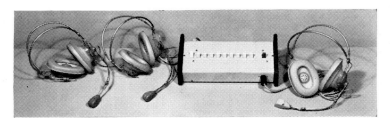

16b The audio-active language laboratory omits individual recording and individual rate-of-learning. On the other hand, at a lower cost and with considerably less demand on space this equipment retains the advantages of direct work with the recorded material and comparison of performance with that of the original.

portant that his deputy should work closely with him. One often finds that control of the laboratory is in the hands of a fairly junior member of the staff. Inevitably the laboratory will share this lack of status. Many decisions involving the language laboratory need to be made at a high administrative level. Not only is the laboratory, and other attendant items of equipment, a large item in a department's financial outlay, the range of work done there and the time-tabling of class and library sessions may call for far-reaching policy decisions.

Ten minutes of drill work is usually enough for a thirty-minute session. Intensive work for a full thirty minutes is usually fairly exhausting. If a class is scheduled for forty minutes this will allow for a full thirty minutes of work as well as the subsequent change-over. Advanced aural comprehension will last longer—usually at least an hour. It is often possible to schedule this work into the laboratory, or parts of the laboratory, as booths are free. The main-tenance of these schedules is important if clashes are to be avoided. If the laboratory session is to be an integral part of the class language learning activities it will need to be set carefully in the weekly pro-gramme for each class.

If the laboratory is not felt to be an integral part of the work there can easily be a breakdown in class cohesion. In this respect the very first laboratory session is important. Headsets should be donned immediately and work should begin straightaway. The machine should be explained in two stages: first, movement of the tape: wind and rewind; secondly, playback and record. Finally, the students should be told to press the 'record' button; respond to the tape; stop the tape, rewind; stop; press playback; stop; rewind; stop; record, and so on. The emphasis must be on their working very intensively. In the first session or two it may be as well to finish early. In all intensive language work the teacher should feel free to call a five-minute or final halt when he senses the end of the students' best effort.

Master tapes (original recordings) must be clearly marked as such and kept well out of the reach of students. It may be as well to have three types of tape:

    master tapes (indelibly marked)
    console tapes (marked in pencil)
    student tapes (marked indelibly if used in a library installation)

Teachers will be making and improving on tapes constantly. Con-sole tapes would give some recognition to early drafts of recorded material, but would encourage continuing revision. In any case tape boxes must show full details of the material on the tape, preferably with tape-counter references. A further list of contents should be indexed and stored elsewhere. No recording should take place without an associated script, and scripts should be kept in a safe place since they offer the quickest guide to points requiring revision.

# CONCLUSION

This book will have achieved its object if the reader is equipped henceforth to discuss the various aspects of contemporary language teaching with more confidence. Whether, at the same time, he emerges from his reading convinced of the all-round value of the new techniques or not, he must recognise that aims and methods are now clearer than they have ever been and that the lines of future development and investigation are there for all to see.

The reader may reject the aims and methods outlined in this book, but only because he prefers the poetry and imprecision of 'educational' or 'cultural' values throughout a course. On the other hand language teachers *are* concerned about the purpose and procedures of the classroom lesson, and the reader of this book will have elected to find out more about his subject. It is to be hoped that he will want to find out still more about one or two of the aspects touched upon in this book. It will be a pity if most teachers choose to remain passive, as the amount of important research in and around language teaching increases. They must know more and say more about work which will eventually produce course material and equipment for *them*.

Work continues at ZAGREB on the production of audio-visual courses on the pattern of the Voix et Images de France course. Psycholinguistic research is carried on at GRENOBLE, and investigations into the teaching of pronunciation are proceeding at the university of MONS. At the Centre de linguistique appliquée of the university of BESANÇON the major part of the work is concerned with lexicology and lexicography, but there is a great deal of work on various aspects of language teaching (these being reported in the irregular publication, *Etudes de linguistique appliquée*). The Bureau d'étude et de liaison (BEL) in PARIS has the responsibility for coordinating some of this effort amongst various of the university institutes in France.

There is some diffuseness in the picture throughout the rest of Western Europe, and even more so, of course, throughout the United States. No indication is available of all the relevant research being carried out by individuals and sections of institutes of the countries of Western Europe other than France and the United Kingdom. Fortunately, some indication of the work in the United States is available through the excellent efforts of the Center for Applied Linguistics in WASHINGTON. Inevitably, major research work tends to centre around certain universities and organisations. There is work attached to the Defense Language Institute and Foreign Service Institute concerned with language learning and material production. The Peace Corps, too, has given an impetus to work on material production and language proficiency testing. The Center for Applied Linguistics is itself concerned with the development of a self-instructional French prototype course. At GEORGETOWN University Professor Lado is investigating 'massive vocabulary expansion in a foreign language beyond the basic course: optimal learning factors and conditions'. Professors Lane and Catford, at the University of MICHIGAN, are carrying out a study of the extension of SAID (Speech Auto-Instructional Device) to segmental features. It is impossible even to begin to summarise the range of work being carried out in the United States.

In Britain work has been slow to develop, although the legacy of Firth in British linguistics has made it easier to associate linguistics and language teaching. An early language laboratory was installed at Ealing Technical College, where in 1962 the Nuffield Foundation backed work on the production of functional courses in (Castilian) Spanish and German. A little later the Nuffield Foundation set up a centre at LEEDS for the production of material in French, Russian and Spanish suitable for the latter years of the primary school and the first years of the secondary school. The production of German material is centred on the University of YORK. At the same time work was started at Leeds on the analysis of child language. In various parts of the country pilot schemes were run by the local authority and the Department of Education to train existing primary school teachers and others with a knowledge of French to use the Leeds material in primary and early secondary classes. The first of these schemes was in fact in Leeds itself. The first of the Nuffield French material from Leeds has been published.

In 1965 the Department of Education and the Nuffield Foundation established the National Committee for Research and Development in Modern Languages (NCRDML), otherwise known as the Farrer-Brown Committee, after the name of its first chairman, the former Director of the Nuffield Foundation. Its work is now very much taken over by a number of sub-committees, each dealing with a particular aspect, such as fundamental research or language-teaching equipment. The National Committee's principal charge is to finance research and development work which will lead to improvements in language teaching. At the same time it is concerned that production shall be matched to defined needs and that there shall be no overlap in work being supported by the limited resources available in Britain. One of the important preliminary investigations carried out at the time the committee was established discovered the language needs of the public services in Great Britain.

The English Teaching Information Centre (ETIC) in London is part of the British Council and, with its library, has for some years provided an excellent service to all those concerned with teaching English as a Foreign Language (EFL), English as a Second Language (EL2) or, as it is often called now, English to Speakers of Other Language (ESOL). Next door to ETIC is the Centre for Information on Language Teaching (CILT) recently established under the aegis of the NCRDML. To a great extent its work will depend on the collaboration of language teacher organisations.

In all countries the language teacher is well supplied with associations, too well supplied. The oldest in Britain is the Modern Language Association (MLA) which, almost because of its long standing, tends to be regarded as an association of teachers of French. Its interests are wider than this, and for many years it displayed an almost exclusive concern with the academic literary aspects of German, Swedish and any other language which came within its purview. Its attitude has recently shown signs of change. Nuffield financed an MLA project to design an examination alternative to 'O' level and this has had its first run. Mainly through its late Honorary Secretary, Dr Presswood, MLA was responsible for the initiative which led to the formation of the Joint Council of Language Associations described below.

Alongside the MLA are the Association of Teachers of German (ATG), of Russian (ATR) and of Spanish (ATSp). The Society for Italian Studies has recently given birth to the Association of Teachers of Italian (ATI).

The Audio-Visual Language Association (AVLA), as its name suggests, was formed at the moment of the audio-visual course (particularly the arrival of *Voix et Images*). Its membership embraces all those interested in the new methods, which might be called the applied linguistic methods of language teaching. The title of AVLA has undergone semantic change, since its interests are by no means restricted to the audio-visual method. AVLA reflects the new unifying direction of language teaching, recognising essentially those things common to all language teaching. Its membership includes a very wide range of languages and represents every possible type of establishment.

Some unity has been brought into language teacher organisations in Britain by the establishment of the Joint Council of Language Associations (JCLA). The first, highly successful, joint conference was held at the University of Leeds in December 1965. Unity of this kind is essential if the interests of all language teachers are to be represented. Inevitably, the universities will be responsible for the relevant research and development work, the results of which will eventually affect the work of every language classroom in the country. The co-operation of teacher associations and the institutes of education can ensure the essential involvement of all stages of language teaching.

The most important and influential of the American language teacher associations, the Modern Language Association of America (MLAA), published in 1955 a useful description of language teacher competence at three levels of proficiency. The MLAA also has a number of language proficiency tests.

The Center for Applied Linguistics is responsible for many aspects of language teaching, co-ordinating and initiating research and the collation of information.

In Britain work at the University of ESSEX includes the collection and analysis of contemporary Russian and the description of different styles or registers of language. At UNIVERSITY COLLEGE, LONDON, there is a full-scale analysis and description of contemporary English usage; the establishment of a programme relating linguistics and the teaching of English as mother-tongue; and the analysis of the linguistic properties of scientific English. A programmed French remedial phonetics course is one of those projected at BIRKBECK COLLEGE, LONDON. Other work which has started at Birkbeck includes a study of effective methods of teaching structure and vocabulary to beginners; the construction and validation of achievement and aptitude tests; and a study of the factors influencing the best rate at which material should be fed to students. At CAMBRIDGE there is work on the elaboration of a functional model for human language behaviour and on the design and production of a full-scale audio-visual and audio-lingual course in Italian using the latest findings of linguistics and psychology. At Cambridge, too, is the Nuffield School Classics Project, which is charged with reconsidering the nature of Latin course material in the light of current linguistic theory.

Prediction is a dangerous pastime, but it is possible to foresee the way language teaching is likely to develop, and indeed matters touched on in this book already foreshadow the probable developments. Equipment will become more reliable and less expensive.

It will take over more of the language teacher's present activities. Eventually the language teacher (and much of this is true of all teaching) will become a producer and director rather than a performer. He will select material on the basis of his assessment of his students' requirements, will carry out frequent testing of progress and will adapt or supplement the course with new material or with remedial material. Most important, his rôle will include the arrangement of 'display' sessions, when the student will be led carefully through use of language he already knows. The display (or 'conversation') session, rather than being viewed as the end of the learning process, will come to be seen as the beginning of language proficiency, for which the rest is preparation.

The equipment will be more flexible. The language laboratory student will select from a number of programmes in accordance with his needs and his aptitude. Multi-programme equipment has been in use at the University of Michigan for a number of years and such equipment should start operation in Britain and elsewhere in the not-too-distant future. At the same time the language laboratory will become less 'blind'. The awareness of the importance of context to language use will encourage the development of visual devices and programmes. The devices might be cartridge-loaded projectors at each student position, or the visual programmes (like the audio programmes) might be available from a central area in the laboratory. But this is looking a long way into the future.

One may look forward to the development of an international exchange of material. Clearly it is easier for the British and Americans to provide examples of English usage, graded linguistically and by purpose, than for each country to assemble or write its own advanced English material. Such material could then be exchanged on a one-to-one basis for material in foreign languages. Schemes of this kind could only function efficiently at national level.

The Council of Europe has long been concerned with standards of language teaching and this has led to the setting up of the Association internationale de linguistique appliquée (AILA) and to the gradual development of national associations. The British Association for Applied Linguistics (BAAL) was formed in 1968.

International co-operation is essential if progress in language teaching is to be ensured. Vertical co-operation—from university to primary school—is no less essential.

# BIBLIOGRAPHY

This list is intended to be short enough to encourage further reading. My aim has been to produce a realistic and basic reading list for all language teachers. I have no doubt omitted some useful books. Nevertheless these will be included in the bibliographies of the books on this present list. Readers will be able to judge the usefulness of books at present omitted by the frequency of their mention in different bibliographies.

CHAPTER I

Background books on language are:

F. de Saussure, *Cours de linguistique générale* (Payot, Paris, 1960).

L. Bloomfield, *Language* (Allen and Unwin, London, 1935).

E. Sapir, *Language, an Introduction to the Study of Speech* (Harcourt Brace, New York, 1921).

De Saussure is often considered as the father of modern linguistics. Certainly his views on language are fundamental to modern investigations into language.

J. R. Firth was the first professor of linguistics at the School of Oriental and African Studies in London University. The major school of contemporary linguistic description in Britain is often called 'Neo-Firthian'. Unfortunately, Firth wrote little, and his views are mainly represented by his former pupils who are now leading figures in contemporary British linguistics. Two brief words which are rewarding reading are *Tongues of Men* and *Speech* which were quite recently republished together (Oxford University Press, 1964).

A book which deals with language in use and misuse is S. I. Hayakawa, *Language in Thought and Action* (Harcourt Brace, New York, 1964). Aspects of language and society are dealt with in *Studies in Sociolinguistics* by A. Capell (Mouton, The Hague, 1966). This is really a book to dip into according to taste, being a collection of widely varied articles.

CHAPTER 2

The best survey of general linguistics is R. H. Robins, *General Linguistics: an introductory survey* (Longmans, 1964). It is not an easy book to read, but it is by far the most comprehensive on the subject available at present.

The concept of the phoneme, undoubtedly one of the most important theories ever suggested, is dealt with very thoroughly in the 'source' book on the subject: D. Jones, *The Phoneme: its Nature and Use* (Heffer, Cambridge, 1950).

Two other works on the phonology of British English are:

A. C. Gimson, *An Introduction to the Pronunciation of English* (Edward Arnold, 1962).

J. D. O'Connor and G. F. Arnold, *Intonation of Colloquial English* (Longmans, 1961).

In many ways the reader is well advised to find out more about his own language, as well as going more deeply into the descriptions of the foreign language he teaches. He is certainly well served if one of these is English. Two books, F. R. Palmer, *A Linguistic Study of the English Verb* (Longmans, 1965), and Barbara Strang, *Modern English Structure* (Edward Arnold, 1962), are both interesting and good examples of the application of new descriptive approaches to British English.

The fundamental work in transformational grammar is Noam Chomsky, *Syntactic Structures* (Mouton, The Hague, 1957). This is very difficult indeed. A readable introduction to the subject is provided by Owen Thomas, *Transformational Grammar and the Teacher of English* (Holt, Rinehart and Winston, 1965). The foundation description of scale and category grammar is M. A. K. Halliday, 'Categories of the Theory of Grammar' (an article to be found in *Word*, 17, no. 3 (1961)). Again, this is difficult reading. An easier presentation is to be found in Halliday's article 'Linguistique générale et linguistique appliquée' in *Etudes de linguistique appliquée*, 1 (Didier, 1962)—an English version of this article is the first paper in *Patterns of Language, Papers in General Descriptive and Applied Linguistics* (Longmans, 1966). *The Linguistic Sciences and Language Teaching* by M. A. K. Halliday, Angus McIntosh and Peter Strevens (Longmans, 1964) is written from the point of view of scale and category grammar.

## CHAPTER 4

B. V. Belayev, *The Psychology of Teaching Foreign Languages* (Pergamon, 1963) is difficult but important. More readable but no less fundamental is the consideration of the assumptions of audio-visual and audio-lingual works by Wilga M. Rivers (*The Psychologist and the Foreign-language Teacher*, University of Chicago Press, 1964). The book by G. A. C. Scherer and Michael Wertheimer, *A Psycholinguistic Experiment in Foreign-language Teaching* (McGraw-Hill, 1964), is less important for its conclusions than for the *way* the experiment was carried out and the number of factors in learning which were measured at the same time.

Programmed learning (including the techniques of programme writing) is dealt with excellently in C. A. Thomas *et al.*, *Programmed Learning in Perspective* (City Publicity Services, 1963) and G. O. M. Leith, E. A. Peel and W. Curr, *A Handbook of Programmed Learning* (University of Birmingham, 1966).

## CHAPTER 5

There are a number of books concerned with language teaching. Fortunately most of them are easy reading. The most specific (not to say dogmatic!) is the teachers' manual which accompanies part 1 of the *Voix et Images* audio-visual course (published by Didier, Paris, and by Harrap in the United Kingdom). Of the others, Nelson Brooks, *Language and*

*Language Learning* (Harcourt Brace, New York, 1964), R. Lado, *Language Teaching, a scientific approach* (McGraw-Hill, 1964), R. Lado, *Linguistics Across Cultures* (University of Michigan Press, 1957) and B. Dutton *et al.*, *Guide to Modern Language Teaching Methods* (Cassell, 1965) are important and readable.

Some idea of the applications of descriptive linguistics to literary work can be found in 'An Approach to the Study of Style' by John Spencer and Michael Gregory in *Linguistics and Style* (Oxford University Press, 1964). The linguistic description in this case is scale and category. The application of transformational-generative grammar to stylistic analysis is touched on in Noam Chomsky's article 'Some Methodological Remarks on Generative Grammar' in *Word*, 17, no. 2 (1961). However this article is extremely difficult.

A delightful essay which considers the linguistic aspects of style in a number of English writers is J. R. Firth 'Modes of Meaning' (in *Essays and Studies*, vol. 4, 1951).

### CHAPTER 6

R. Lado, *Language Testing* (Longmans, 1961) is the most comprehensive work on the subject. It is a very clear account, written principally from the point of view of item testing. The manual accompanying the *Modern Language Aptitude Test* of J. B. Carroll and S. H. Sapon (Psychological Corp., New York, 1959, in U.K.: National Foundation for Educational Research) includes an interesting account of the validation of this widely recognised battery of tests.

### CHAPTER 7

Robert Lado's *Language Teaching* deals with types of material and their function, as does the book by E. M. Stack mentioned below. Types of drill material are considered in B. Woolrich, 'Writing Language Laboratory and Classroom Drills' (*English Language Teaching*, Oxford University Press, 19, 2 January 1965) and Ruth Hok, 'Oral Exercises: their Type and Form' in *Modern Language Journal* (vol. XLVIII, 4, 1964). A very thorough description of drill types is given by S. P. Kaczmarski in 'Language Drills and Exercises—a Tentative Classification' (*International Review of Applied Linguistics*, Heidelberg, III/3, 1965).

Some of the contrasts which suggest where difficulties may occur for the language learner are given in books of the *Contrastive Structure Series* published by the University of Chicago Press on behalf of the Center for Applied Linguistics, Washington. Titles so far available are:

*The Sounds of English and German*, W. G. Moulton (1962).
*The Grammatical Structures of English and German*, H. L. Kufner (1962).
*The Sounds of English and Spanish*, R. P. Stockwell and J. D. Bowen (1965).
*The Grammatical Structures of English and Spanish*, R. P. Stockwell J. D. Bowen and J. W. Martin (1965).

*The Sounds of English and Italian*, F. B. Agard and R. J. di Pietro (1965).
*The Grammatical Structures of English and Italian*, F. B. Agard and R. J. di Pietro (1965).

These books deal with only part of the topic each time, and some linguists would disagree with parts of the analysis used. More important, remember that they deal with *American* English. Further volumes will deal with French and Russian.

A list of course material is published by Visual Education National Information Service for Schools (VENISS), Educational Foundation for Visual Aids (EFVA), 33 Queen Anne Street, London, W. 1.

## CHAPTER 8

E. J. P. Devereux (ed.), *An Introduction to Visual Aids* (Visual Aids Centre, London, 1962), Margaret Simpson, *Film Projecting Without Tears or Technicalities* (EFVA, 1960), R. S. Judd, *Teaching by Projection* (Focal Press, 1963), John Weston, *The Tape Recorder in the Classroom* (EFVA, 1963) and manuals, such as that produced for the tape-recorder by Grundig, provide a very good coverage of the technical aspects of various types of equipment.

For those faced with the larger decisions attendant upon language laboratory purchase A. S. Hayes, *Language Laboratory Facilities* (U.S. Department of Education OE-21024, 1963) is an excellent explanation of its technical aspects. The first book to deal satisfactorily with technical, administrative and methodological aspects of the language laboratory was E. M. Stack, *The Language Laboratory and Modern Language Teaching* (Oxford University Press). Originally published in 1960, a revised edition appeared in 1966. The only regret one might have is that its wide popularity at its first appearance gave rise to the damaging assumption that the language laboratory is fundamental to the new methods of language teaching. This is just not so.

For those who want to keep in touch with developments in the subjects covered in this book, as far as they touch upon language teaching, no periodical at present surpasses the *International Review of Applied Linguistics* (IRAL), published by Julius Groos Verlag, Heidelberg. Increasingly valuable, too, is the *AVLA Journal*, free to members of the Audio-Visual Language Association. The Center for Applied Linguistics in Washington distributes, at nominal cost, the very interesting *Linguistic Reporter*, containing a lot of useful information about books, material and research on and around language teaching.

*Visual Education*, published by the Educational Foundation for Visual Aids, has much of interest to modern language teachers, although, of course, it deals with the whole range of aural and visual aids in education. *Le Français dans le monde* (Hachette) is a review which reflects much of the new methods, although it is, of course, largely concerned with the re-quirements of teachers of French.

Readers who would like to keep up to date with articles on linguistics which may appear in the more esoteric magazines will find it useful to be on the mailing list of the Bobbs-Merrill Co. Ltd, 4300 West 62nd Street, Indianapolis 6, Indiana, USA who publish in a cheap, attractive and handy form reprints of the most important articles on general linguistics.

# GLOSSARY

*Allomorph:* a variant within a class of inflexions; the variations are without significance. In English, for instance, '-ed' '-en' and zero are possible allomorphs of the past participle morpheme.

*Allophone:* a variant within a class of segmental sounds; the variations are without significance, being conditioned by the preceding and subsequent sounds. Thus, in English, the initial 'k' of kick /kik/ is different from the 'c' of cock /kɔk/. The two sounds are allophones of the phoneme /k/.

*Audio-active:* an arrangement whereby the sound picked up by a microphone is amplified and fed back to the earphones of the speaker. Also used of a language laboratory system in which the student does not have a separate recording facility.

*Basic sentence types:* sentence patterns to which all sentences in the language can be reduced. One type common to English may be exemplified by: 'He posted the letter at the corner.'

*Bilingualism:* the possession of two languages to a native degree of competence in each. (The term 'ambilingualism' is sometimes retained for the possession of two languages from earliest childhood.)

*Branching programme:* a programme in which alternative routes are provided in accordance with the student's performance at each stage.

*Bulk eraser:* a device for demag-netising by means of one electrical charge, thus saving time otherwise needed to pass each tape in front of an erase head on a tape player.

*Cline:* a continuous connexion between levels of analysis, of such a kind that it cannot be broken into separate units. Delicacy in scale and category grammar is considered as being a cline since the only *discrete* (separate) degrees of delicacy are those of most delicate and least delicate. Any statement of delicacy between these poles is necessarily artificial.

*Co-text:* the total linguistic environment of a linguistic event; to be distinguished from context.

*Collocation:* the co-occurrence of linguistic forms; usually restricted to statements about lexical items.

*Comparative linguistics:* the comparison of the linguistic features of two or more languages.

*Console:* the teacher's desk in the language laboratory, with switchboard and programme sources.

*Constructed response:* the student's contribution to the response in a frame of a programme; usually by completion with one word.

*Context:* the non-linguistic environment of a linguistic event.

*Degausser/Demagnetiser:* a device for removing the unwanted magnetic charge which builds up in the heads of a tape-recorder.

*Dialect:* the total of linguistic

*Dialect (cont.)*
variants in one region of a speech-community from the forms in any other region; dialects are mutually intelligible.

*Dual-channel tape-recorder:* a machine arranged for the recording or replay of two tracks simultaneously (also called 'stereophonic').

*Dubbing:* sometimes used to describe the process of transferring a recording from one machine to another (copying) or from console to student machines (transferring).

*Erase head:* the source of an electric charge (on a tape-recorder) sufficient to cancel the recording on a tape passed in front of it.

*Extensive listening/Extensive reading:* listening/reading for the purpose of gaining a general understanding of the text (in contrast with listening/reading for a deep understanding).

*Favourite sentences:* those basic sentence types which are common to most sentences in the language and which serve as the basis for most sentences generated in the language.

*Feedback:* the return of an output: it may be the reaction of a listener or learner to a unit of information or stimulation; it may be the electrical amplification of an electrical output (resulting in a whine from a tape-recorder).

*Filmloop:* a continuous loop of (usually) 8 mm film which can be handled in a cartridge (also called 'cineloop').

*Filmstrip:* a short length of (usually) 35 mm film, of which the frames may be shown separately or as a sequence.

*Form words:* nouns, verbs, adjectives, etc., which provide the substance of a sentence. For example, in the English sentence 'The Minister of Education will speak tomorrow' the form words are 'Minister Education speak tomorrow' (cf. structure words).

*Four-track recording:* the provision of two record and two replay heads, one above the other, in such a way that two tracks may be used in one direction and then a further two when the tape is turned over.

*Frame:* a unit of a film, filmstrip (picture) or teaching programme. In 35 mm filmstrip the frame

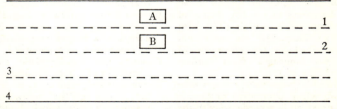

Fig. 17. Tracks are, course, the paths followed by the heads—not paths marked out on the tape. Tracks 3 and 4 in the diagram are the paths which will be followed by heads *A* and *B* when the tape has been turned over.

*Frame (cont.)*
measures 36 × 24 mm. Some filmstrips (and some cameras) work with half-frames (18 × 24 mm) thus doubling the number of frames to a length of film. There is a tendency to standardise with 18 × 24 mm frames as the norm, referring to the 36 × 24 mm as a double frame.

*Frequency response:* the range of sound which a machine will accurately reproduce. It is measured in *cycles per second* (c.p.s.).

Fig. 18. Full-track recording.

*Full-track recording:* the head sits squarely against the centre of the tape. It is, therefore, not possible to turn the tape over and record on another track. There is no justification in this doubling of tape costs outside the most delicate of professional work. There used to be concern that the tape tension might not be consistently maintained between the loaded spool and the take-up spool, that the tape might droop and the head thus record on a part of the tape already recorded in the other direction. There is no longer a danger of this happening with a reputable machine. Professional sound engineers express the same doubts, however, about the four-track machine—possibly with some justification at the present time.

*Gain control:* the technical term for what is called by mortals 'volume control'.

*Half-frame:* see *Frame*.

*Head-word:* the syntactically dominant word in each group; the word which would be left when all the others had been removed on grammatical (*not* semantic) grounds. Thus in 'The old man sat down' the head-words are 'man' and 'sat'.

*Historical linguistics:* the study of a language through the stages of its development. In this it may be contrasted with comparative linguistics. The former is concerned with the comparison of two or more stages of the same language; the latter compares two or more languages at the same stage. The development of a language is, of course, continuous, so that any description of it at a certain *stage* is bound to be to that extent artificial.

*Immediate constituents:* the components of language when it is taken as a stream of substance, phonic or graphic.

*Intensive listening/Intensive reading:* listening/reading for full understanding; concentration on a limited text.

*I.P.A.:* the phonetic transcription system of the International Phonetic Association.

*Item testing:* the testing of control of specific linguistic items 'In that field, is that a ship /ʃip/ or a sheep /ʃiːp/?'

*Juncture:* word boundary marked by a pause or other phonetic variation.

*Leader tape:* coloured tape attached to the end of magnetic item. It

*Leader tape* (*cont.*)
serves to protect the end of the magnetic tape when the tape is laced to the take-up spool and its colours can be used to indicate which tracks are being used. It may be used at various points in the tape to indicate the beginning of different material. It is essential that leader film be attached to the beginning of film and filmstrip to prevent damage.

*Level control:* the presetting of volume by means of a meter.

*Lexical item:* one or more words functioning as a group and assignable to no part of the grammar.

*Lexis:* the component of language (in both graphology and phonology) which is not grammar.

*Library mode:* the use of the language laboratory for individual study.

*Listen-respond:* the simplest language laboratory arrangement in which the student merely responds into the air, having no audio-active headset nor any recording facility.

*Linear programme:* a programme of material in which units of material (steps) are so small that error may be discounted (5 per cent error is generally regarded as acceptable). All students proceed through the same steps, unless led to skip a number of steps in a *skip-frame* or forward-branching programme. Typical of the linear programme is the constructed response rather than the multiple-choice response.

*Morpheme:* the smallest meaningful unit of language. A word may be in itself a *free* morpheme; a *bound* morpheme can only exist as part of a word. In the word 'encouragement' there are two *bound* morphemes 'en-' and '-ment' and one free morpheme 'courage'. 'Morpheme', like 'phoneme', is sometimes used to refer to a class of these smallest units between which there is no significant difference because no option is possible. Thus in 'impossible', 'unthinkable' and 'non-toxic', 'im-', 'un-' and 'non-' are not interchangeable and may be regarded as allomorphs of the one bound morpheme of negation.

*Morphology:* the system of formal variants within a language and their relationship with other aspects of that language. The study of this system.

*Morphophonology* (or *morphonology*): relationship which exists between the morphology and phonology of a language.

*Multiple-choice:* a number of possible responses from which the student selects one.

*Non-favourite sentence:* types of sentence which are not common in a language. In English, for instance, 'needs must' is unique as a sentence pattern (we cannot produce 'dares must' or 'does must').

*Operant conditioning:* the behaviouristic theory of learning associated with B. F. Skinner in which the response (elicited no matter how from all the possibilities) is instrumental to the learning.

*Paradigmatic:* the (vertical) re-

*Paradigmatic (cont.)*
lationship between linguistic items which are mutually interchangeable at one place within the sentence structure (regardless of resultant changes in lexical meaning within the whole structure).

*Pause button:* a temporary stop on a tape-recorder, of great importance in language teaching.

*Phoneme:* a class of sounds within which variants are conditioned solely by the phonological environment and have no significance outside the sound system.

*Phonology:* the system in which sound is organised in a language, both the selection of certain sounds from the far greater range of possibilities and the interrelationship of these sounds.

*Playback head:* a device in a tape-recorder which detects changes in the magnetic field on the tape. The resulting current is then amplified and converted to sound.

*Psycholinguistics:* the study of the relationship between mental processes and the use or learning of language. It is concerned, also, with questions of visual and aural perception.

*Radio jack:* a simple radio receiver built on to a plug.

*Record head:* the device on a tape-recorder which converts sound to an electrical current which in turn sets up a corresponding magnetic field on the tape.

*Redundancy:* the degree of predictability of any linguistic item as a result of context (Phew, it's...) or co-text (I'm feeling old and...).

*Register:* the total variation in linguistic features within one social (not geographical) area from the total of variations in any other social area.

*Replay head:* see *Playback head*.

*Rewind:* the transport of tape from right to left (i.e. from end to beginning).

*Scale and category grammar:* see chapter 2.

*Segment:* a small constituent. Applied to pronunciation it refers to the smallest unit of completed sound. The English word 'ticket' consists of five *segmental* sounds /tikət/. The term also used sometimes to refer to the lowest level of morphological analysis. Thus 'struck' may be said to have two segments str-(c)k.

*Semantics:* the study of meaning from a conceptual rather than a formal point of view.

*Sociolinguistics:* the study of the relationship between language and social structure.

*Splicing tape:* tape for joining lengths of magnetic tape when editing or when the tape has been broken.

*Structure words:* prepositions, conjunctions and auxiliary verbs, etc., which link *form words* in a meaningful sequence. In the English sentence 'The Minister of Education will speak tomorrow' the structure words are 'the of will'.

*Style:* conscious individual variations from the norm or contrasts with the linguistic co-text. In written language it may be the mark of literary effort; in the spoken language it may more

*Style (cont.)*
> commonly have a largely social function. (The linguistic study of literary texts is often given the name of 'Stylistics' or 'Linguostylistics'.)

*Suprasegmental:* used solely in one approach to the analysis of phonology. If segmental analysis deals with the smallest complete sound, suprasegmental analysis deals with the questions of stress, intonation and juncture.

*Syntagmatic:* the horizontal relationship between the linguistic items within the sentence structure and between sentences.

*Syntax:* the meaningful sequential relationship of linguistic items in time or space ('word order').

*Take-up spool:* the spool to which the leader tape is laced on a tape-recorder.

*Tape deck:* the top of the tape-recorder; it is often out of sight in the student booth of a language laboratory.

*Tape speed:* there is a direct relationship between sound quality and tape speed. Sound engineers are beginning to work with 7½ i.p.s. (19 cm/sec), a reflexion of improved tape quality. *Some* machines are capable of accurately reproducing a sufficient range of sound for language work at 3¾ i.p.s. (9.5 cm/sec) but not many.

*Transformational-generative grammar:* see chapter 2.

*Utterance:* in the search for points of reference linguists have attempted to specify this unit, with particular reference to the spoken language. It seems of less value than the equally indeterminate 'sentence' as the basis of linguistic description and operation. It is often used to refer to a passage of continuous spoken or written language (text). In this book it is coterminous with 'sentence' as the smallest stretch of context-related language events.

*Voice:* the addition of vibration of the vocal chords to the articulation of a sound. In English, unlike many languages, the addition of voice is phonemic, distinguishing words like 'tug' and 'dug'; 'tuck' and 'tug'.

# INDEX